THE MADE-FROM-SCRATCH LIFE

MELISSA K. NORRIS

TEN PEAKS PRESS®
EUGENE, OR

To my husband,
who has fully embraced this way of life and my forays into making
everything from scratch (even the flops), and supported my dream of
being a writer when I didn't believe in myself.
This wouldn't be possible without you.

Published in association with the literary agency of WordServe Literary Group, Ltd., www.wordserveliterary.com.

Cover and interior design by Dugan Design Group. Cover photo and photo on page 224 by Jay Eads.

Household themed graphics © Olga / Adobe Stock; gardening themed graphics © ONYXprj / Adobe Stock; kitchen themed graphics © Fredy Sujono / Adobe Stock; canning themed graphics © m.malinika / Adobe Stock; animal themed graphics © ihork / Adobe Stock; vegetable, fruit, herb and berry themed graphics © Baksiabat / Creative Market

TEN PEAKS PRESS is a federally registered trademark of the Hawkins Children's LLC. Harvest House Publishers, Inc., is the exclusive licensee of this trademark.

TEN PEAKS PRESS®

The Garlic Dill Pickles recipe originally appeared in *Everything Worth Preserving* by Melissa K. Norris © 2023. Used by permission of Homestead Living.

Some material previously published in *The Family Garden Plan* and *The Family Garden Planner*.

The Made-from-Scratch Life

Copyright © 2016, 2023 by Melissa K. Norris

Published by Harvest House Publishers
Eugene, Oregon 97408
www.harvesthousepublishers.com

ISBN 978-0-7369-8722-6 (hardcover)
ISBN 978-0-7369-8723-3 (eBook)

Library of Congress Control Number: 2023935000

Printed in China

23 24 25 26 27 28 29 30 31 / RDS / 10 9 8 7 6 5 4 3 2 1

CONTENTS

CHAPTER 1

GROW

Remain in me, as I also remain in you. No branch can bear fruit by itself; it must remain in the vine. Neither can you bear fruit unless you remain in me. I am the vine; you are the branches. If you remain in me and I in you, you will bear much fruit; apart from me you can do nothing.

JOHN 15:4-5

Growing your own food is rewarding on so many levels. I think everyone should try to grow some of their own food. You may not have been born into a gardening family, but I promise you, you can become a gardener. Of course there's a learning curve, and there might be frustrations along the way. In fact, I'd be surprised if you don't run into some sort of conundrum. Anything worth doing will make you forge on ahead and over problems, and gardening is no different. This chapter contains my best tips for helping to curb those pitfalls as much as possible. Like anything in life, you'll continue to learn more every year you garden.

Each area and climate zone will have its own unique challenges and requirements. We won't cover everything here that you may come up against, but this will give you a good base and hopefully highlight areas for seasoned gardeners to look at as well.

☙

While God has met me in many places, I feel a special nearness to Him when I'm working in my garden. When life feels dark, I am reminded that God is already at work beneath the dormancy, preparing new seeds and new growth for the right time. And when there is joy, God's promises sprout right alongside the new shoots emerging from rich soil. I am assured that He is our master gardener, and our life rhythms are like the seasons of nature: we must pass through each one before we can enter the next.

I am also reminded how His plan of nourishment and provision through what we grow is a legacy intended to continue for generations.

My family has been saving and passing down our own strain of green pole bean for over a hundred years, near as we can trace.

When my father was five years old, he and my grandparents migrated from the Appalachian Mountains of North Carolina to the steep slopes of the Pacific Northwest. With two other families, they converted an old truck into a camper and headed out. It took a little over a week of travel to make it to Washington. My grandfather found work in the woods as a logger, and my grandmother set about making their home with the meager supplies they'd brought west. Tucked into those belongings was a small seed, just as big as your fingernail, white and smooth. But from this one small seed God created enough food to feed their family through the winter months. From this one seed, God created enough food to feed uncountable families for decades to come.

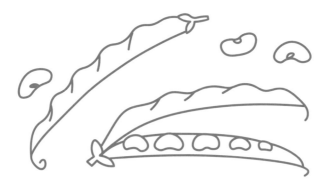

The seed was that of a Tarheel green pole bean. These green beans are a heritage (or heirloom) bean. At the time of my grandparents' migration, there wasn't such a thing as hybrid seed on the market yet. Genetically modified foods weren't something anyone would have fathomed.

This is beautiful to me. The seed doesn't cost a thing. When planted, it produces enough food to feed your family, and as it dies it provides you with the means to do it all over again. You see, God knew what He was doing when He created this world. Nature was made to work in balance. It's when we mess with it that things get off-kilter.

MAKING YOUR GARDEN FROM SCRATCH

Learning to grow a garden is one of the most rewarding things my family and I do. We are able to cut back on our food bill, eat healthier, become more self-sustaining, teach our children a strong work ethic, and observe the incredible way God created nature to work in rhythm.

Did you know that food grown at home has more nutrients and vitamins than produce bought at the store, farmers' markets, or even Community Supported Agriculture (CSA) programs? When food is allowed to ripen on the vine, it develops more nutrients and vitamins than early-harvested crops. Once it's picked, it begins to lose those nutrients and vitamins.

Food we purchase in the store is picked before it's fully ripe to allow for shipping time and the time it sits out on the shelf. It doesn't have a chance to fully develop its nutrients. Although farmers' markets are local and don't require as much shipping time, they still take some. CSAs usually deliver once a week during the harvest months, but even then, you won't be eating food straight from the vine.

When you grow your food at home, you pick it and prepare it immediately. No time for it to lose its nutrients and vitamins. It's also amazing to taste the difference between vine-ripened, just-picked food, and vegetables that have been shipped halfway across the country or world.

Some of you may be thinking, *I don't have enough acreage or a huge yard to grow a big garden.* That's okay. Even if all you have is a windowsill, you can still grow some of your own food. Even if you don't own any land or don't have any yard space, many communities now offer up gardening space in a community garden. You can also do container gardening on a patio, porch, or deck. You can plant a small windowsill herb garden.

The first thing you need to do is commit to gardening for at least one season. Deciding to do something, instead of just thinking about it, is half the battle. Enlist the help of your family and make it something you all do together.

Choosing Your Garden Site

Choose your garden spot wisely. You'll want to make sure the place you choose has adequate sunlight. Most plants require at least six hours of sunlight. Shade-tolerant plants—greens and short-season crops like radishes—will usually perform with less sunlight while your tomatoes and peppers will require more. Most fruit and vegetables will do best with full sun. When choosing your site, remember that trees that are bare in winter will provide more shade when their leaves come out in spring and summer. Tall buildings will cast less shade in the summer months when the angle of the sun is higher.

Consider how close you are to your water supply. If you're carrying water by hand, you don't want to haul it too far. If you're using sprinklers or drip hoses, you don't want to

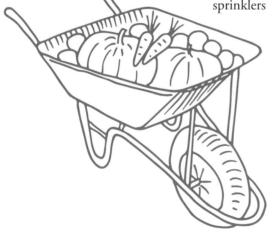

have to run miles of hoses or have to move them every time you mow the lawn.

Look at the slope of the ground. In a heavy rainstorm, will all the water run down and pool in your garden? A level area is preferable so you don't have water pooling. Look for natural windbreaks if possible. Wind can batter tender or tall plants, dry the plants and soil, and cause erosion.

Avoiding some of these pitfalls will make your gardening easier. Remember, though, that there are ways to make a garden work on some level no matter what your conditions are. If you lack the perfect spot, don't let it deter you from putting in a garden. Work with what you have.

Creating a New Garden Bed

Fall is the ideal time to create a new in-ground garden bed, but it can be done any time of year. The first thing to do is clear the area of competing plant matter, usually grass. This can be accomplished in two ways. I find it most effective to use both methods together.

Go over the area with a rototiller. You can rent them from many hardware or garden centers or maybe a neighbor has one you can borrow. This type of tilling on existing lawn/pasture will only break up the root wads of the grass for easier removal, it won't turn over deep layers of soil on the first pass through of unbroken ground. Some people prefer a no-till approach, but even in no-till beds, we still use this approach when initiating a new bed. It also helps aerate the soil.

After the first pass through, take a rake and remove any large clumps of grass and roots. Once you've removed the large clumps, you need to cover the soil. Contrary to what you would think, clear plastic will heat up faster than black plastic. Clear plastic applied in the summer will effectively kill weeds within two to three weeks; during cooler months, it may take a few months. Black plastic will get the job done but can take up to six weeks in summer and six months over fall/winter.

Even if you don't have access to a tiller, you can still use solarization to kill plants in a plot to create a garden bed.

Soil and Compost

After choosing your garden spot, you'll want to look at your soil. Is it sandy, rocky, or primarily clay? Does it drain well? Knowing what kind of soil you have will help you know how to amend it. Most soil will benefit from the addition of some good organic matter. Your plants are living things and need good food in order to grow and produce. This can be from a compost pile, aged and dried-out manure (not fresh), or even fertilizer purchased from the store. Seed meal, feather meal, and bagged manure make good fertilizer to grow healthy plants.

Manure from any animal will work. Chicken, cow, horse, llama or alpaca manure, and rabbit manure are most common. The key is to turn and cover the manure. If used when fresh, the seed of whatever the animal has been eating may begin to grow in your garden area. Fresh manure is oftentimes too hot or has too much nitrogen in it, and it can kill your plants if it is applied directly to the roots (rabbit manure being an exception, it can be applied fresh without issue). Mix the manure with some straw or sawdust, cover it, and allow it to sit for a few months before applying it to your garden. This works especially well if done in the fall (hot weather can make the smell a bit more unpleasant), and by the time spring planting comes around, it will be ready to be mixed into the soil.

The heat from composting microbes working to decompose the organic material is what kills the weed seeds. To make sure this happens, you'll need the right ratio of carbon and nitrogen. The best ratio for a beginning compost pile is 30 parts carbon to 1 part nitrogen by weight. Carbon materials are often referred to as brown and include wood chips, dry leaves, cardboard, and branches. Nitrogen materials are referred to as greens and include grass clippings, manure from cattle, sheep, goats, and chickens, and fruit and vegetable scraps. It is not advised to use dairy, meat, or fat scraps as these can attract unwanted pests.

Keeping this pile moist and turning it often will help keep temperatures high enough to kill the weed seeds. Your soil will also benefit from the addition of seed meal and even alfalfa hay.

While the pH level of your soil is important and we're going to discuss it a little bit here, it's not as important as having well fed soil. Most plants will still grow in soil that leans slightly one way or the other—acidic or alkaline. For example, we successfully grew broccoli, cabbage, and brussels sprouts in our acidic soil long before I knew they preferred a more neutral pH of 6.5.

However, knowing the acidity level of your soil can help you troubleshoot and grow a more successful garden. If your pH levels are too far off, it can affect the plant's ability to take in nutrients, eventually killing them (blueberries are a great example of this). Living in the Pacific Northwest, our soil is generally on the slightly acidic side. This works well for blueberries, raspberries, and potatoes, as well as most vegetables. However, beets and *Brassicas* like more neutral soil.

Before amending your soil, especially for pH levels, you should perform a soil test. You need to know the exact level so you can accurately apply the correct amendments.

Ideally, a soil test will analyze:

1. PH Level (the optimal range is 6.0 to 7.0 for vegetable gardens)
2. Nitrogen (nitrate-N)
3. Phosphorus (P)
4. Potassium (K)
5. Calcium (Ca)
6. Magnesium (Mg)
7. Boron (B)
8. Sulfur (S)
9. Organic Matter
10. Zinc (Zn)
11. Manganese (Mn)
12. Copper (Cu)
13. Iron (Fe)
14. Sodium (Na)

I live in Washington state, which is one of the few places that doesn't offer testing through the county extension office. Instead, I use a mail-in soil testing service with a lab. Both SimplySoilTesting.com and Redmond Agriculture.com offer easy, affordable kits that will return your lab results in days.

How to Perform a Soil Test for Accurate Results

Fall is an ideal time to test because you have the full winter months to allow the amendments to incorporate into the soil. However, you can still test in early spring. You want at least four weeks between making the amendments and planting to allow the soil to absorb the changes you made and have the nutrients readily available to the plants.

Your soil results are only going to be as good as your sample.

1. Grab a clean container to put your dirt into. A 5-gallon bucket works well.
2. Pick at least six spots evenly spaced over the entire area of your garden. A good rule of thumb is to use a W pattern, taking a sample from each point of the W and then one additional spot.
3. Use a spade or shovel and get soil from 6 to 8 inches deep and place this in your container.
4. Place all six soil samples into the container and mix them together thoroughly.
5. Place one cup of the mixed soil into a sealed container. (Or follow the instructions from the soil sampling company; some will say to dry out the soil first.)
6. Properly label your soil sample container. If you're doing multiple tests for different gardens or beds, make sure each sample is properly labeled, and retain your records on which soil sample goes with each gardening bed.
7. Send off your sample and wait for the results, then amend the soil as needed. To amend acidic soil, you can add wood ash or lime. If it's too alkaline and you need it to be more acidic, you can use elemental sulfur or coffee grounds.

When lowering the pH level of your soil to make it more acidic, use caution! Never lower it more than one level on the pH scale in a given year. Take care to read the instructions on the sulfur you use to make sure you don't apply too much. If needed, do two applications over the year instead of adding it all at once. This is a slow, long-term process. Have patience and be the turtle here, not the hare.

If your soil is too acidic and you need to make it more alkaline, use lime or calcium. There are varying points of view on using lime (made from crushed limestone) versus ground-up oyster shells (for calcium, see page 42 for more options). Both will increase alkalinity. If your soil already has a high magnesium level, use the ground-up oyster shells instead of lime. You can also use wood ash to raise the alkalinity of your soil.

Whichever of the above-mentioned soil amendments you use, it's best to work it into the top six inches of soil. It is not as efficient to do a simple top dressing where you just sprinkle it on.

There are lots of at-home soil test kits, and most county extension offices will test soil for you as well. A soil test eliminates guessing and allows you to provide the exact elements your soil needs to create a healthy foundation for your plants and ecosystem.

Coffee Grounds and Soil Acidity

Do coffee grounds increase soil acidity? This is an area of great debate with gardeners. The short answer is no—used coffee grounds will not significantly change the pH level of your soil. However, coffee grounds can be a great soil builder and a natural fertilizer. A study done by a lab for *Sunset* magazine has a great break down of how coffee grounds improve your soil. Most notable are the phosphorus, potassium, magnesium, and copper levels.[1]

I have used grounds for years on my blueberries, raspberries, and tomatoes. These tips will help you choose when and how to use those java remains:

1. Some studies show used coffee grounds to have a medium level of acidity, while others put them at only slightly acidic. Any time you're amending your soil you'll want to start with a small amount. You can always add more, but you can't take it back out.
2. Make sure you spread them out in a thin layer and work them into the soil or mulch.

---

1 "Add Used Coffee Grounds to Your Garden Soil and Get Amazing Results," *Sunset*, June 26, 2006, https://www.sunset.com/garden/earth-friendly/starbucks-coffee-compost-test.

3. Aim to keep the coffee grounds to 25 to 35 percent of the total volume when mixing them in with your mulch or soil.

4. Wet grounds will clump together and can develop mold as well as create a barrier that keeps out the moisture and air your soil needs.

5. If you don't want to deal with changing the pH level of your soil, then simply pick the plant varieties that naturally grow well with your soil's pH level. Most plants will get along fine with pH levels between 5.5 and 7. There are some exceptions to this generality (aren't there always) so I've listed out the plants below that really need more acidic soil to grow well.

Fruits and Vegetables That Prefer Highly Acidic Soil

Acidic soil is 0 to 6.9 pH level, with 4.5 to 5.5 being considered highly acidic.

Blueberries (they are one of the most acid-loving plants out there)	Cranberries	Potatoes
	Currants	Rhubarb
	Elderberries	Raspberries
	Peppers	

Fruits and Vegetables That Prefer Alkaline Soil

Alkaline or sweet basic soil is 7.1 to 10 pH level.

Asparagus	Leeks	Parsnips
Beets	Marjoram	

Choosing What to Plant

My best advice when gardening is to start out simple. It's tempting and fun to go through seed catalogs and walk through the produce aisles of the grocery store dreaming about growing all you see there. Most of us would love to cut back on our grocery bill, and growing your own food certainly does help with that. When we're plunking seedlings or seeds into that soil, it doesn't look like all that much. But when all those plants start to grow and require more care, you'll begin to wonder what on earth you were thinking.

Start by planting foods you and your family eat a lot and that grow well

in your region. For example, here in the Pacific Northwest I can't successfully grow okra, sweet potatoes, or peanuts. The weather simply isn't hot enough for those plants. Peppers and tomatoes tend to do best with a greenhouse here, though they can be grown outdoors (depending on the summer). Peppers and tomatoes will flourish in the south or in hotter areas, but beets and snow peas might not fare as well there.

Most seed catalogs and seed packets will specify an ideal region or climate zone. Getting advice from someone who has gardened successfully in your region is important. They will know from experience and be able to guide you. You can also get a lot of advice from a local independent nursery. They've been quite helpful when we were trying to decide which varieties of apple trees and strawberries to put in. Many of them will also have seedlings of vegetables known to do well in your specific zone and region.

Another way we select what to plant is by how well the item can be preserved. While cucumbers are most people's go-to for pickling, my husband really doesn't care for cucumber pickles. However, we've been known to eat an entire quart of pickled asparagus at one meal. My daughter has grown to love cucumber pickles, especially fermented garlic dill pickles (see page 114 for the recipe), so we grow the 'Chicago Pickling' cucumber. It's a prolific producer that is enjoyable fresh on salads, and it makes great pickles.

We plant some lettuce because we love fresh salads, but we don't want a lot left over. Frozen lettuce isn't that appealing unless you're using it in a green smoothie. We choose to grow more kale and spinach, both of which can be frozen and used in various dishes.

Each family is unique and it's important to remember to tailor what you grow in accordance with what your family prefers to eat. Don't worry if you start out small, thinking it won't be enough. Being able to stay on top of a small garden will have you eager to plant more next year. Every year we bring in one new vegetable or variety to try. Usually that means we end up enlarging our garden plot bit by bit as well. Working new ground and just planting cover crops the first year is a great way to get your soil ready for new vegetables. It helps reduce the weeds, lets old sod break down, and builds organic matter. There are lots of reasons to expand slowly.

GROW A YEAR'S WORTH OF FOOD FOR YOUR FAMILY

To determine how much and what you should be planting for your family, I'm including these charts, shared from *The Family Garden Plan*.[2]

This family garden planning guide will show you how to grow healthy, organic fruits, vegetables, and herbs year-round. The following worksheets will help you determine what your family's produce needs are, how much you should plant, and how to plan your garden space accordingly.

No matter your climate, conditions, and space, you can grow crops that will help reduce your grocery budget and provide wholesome and chemical-free food, improving your and your family's overall well-being.

Ready to grow? Start here.

How To Use These Worksheets

These sheets will help you accomplish one of the often most overlooked but critical steps to a successful growing season and harvest—planning.

First, you'll determine your food needs for a year by identifying the produce your family eats and enjoys during a typical month. After all, what's the point of having a garden if it's full of foods your family doesn't like and won't eat?

Next, you'll need to do some research to determine which of the foods your family eats will grow in the climate where you live. To search online for your gardening zone information, type your zip code or city into the search tool with the words "average first and last frost date" or "gardening zone." If possible, it's also wise to ask an experienced gardener in your area.

Finally, you'll take the information you gathered about your family's food needs and what grows well in your area to determine what and how much to plant. This will give you an easy-to-follow plan for your garden and provide enough yield to feed your family for a year. There is also graph paper provided (pages 26-28), so you can sketch out how your garden area will look.

Here's to a great growing year for you and your family!

---

2 Melissa K. Norris, *The Family Garden Plan* (Eugene: Harvest House Publishers, 2020).

FOOD NEEDS FOR A YEAR WORKSHEET

This worksheet will help you to document and plan out approximate yearly needs based on your family's eating habits.

Food	Serving Amount Per Meal	Week 1	Week 2	Week 3	Week 4	Weekly Average	Yearly Need
	2 cups, 1 pound, etc.	Serving amount x meals	Serving amount x meals	Serving amount x meals	Serving amount x meals	Total serving amounts divided by 4 weeks	Average weekly use x 52 weeks
green beans	2 cups	2x2= 4 cups	2x0= 0 cups	2x1= 2 cups	2x0= 0 cups	6 cups/ 4 weeks= 1 1/2 cups	1 1/2 cups x 52 weeks = 78 cups

Food	Serving Amount Per Meal	Week 1	Week 2	Week 3	Week 4	Weekly Average	Yearly Need
	2 cups, 1 pound, etc.	Serving amount x meals	Serving amount x meals	Serving amount x meals	Serving amount x meals	Total serving amounts divided by 4 weeks	Average weekly use x 52 weeks

GROWING SEASON WORKSHEET

1. My gardening zone is _____.
2. My last average frost date is _____.
3. My first average frost date is _____.
4. My growing season is _____ days .

Crop Planning Worksheet

Now that you know which foods your family is eating a lot of, it's time to decide which of these crops you'll be planting in your garden this year. Consider what crops grow easily in your zone.

Annual Vegetables	Perennial Vegetables	Fruits	Herbs
zucchini	asparagus	raspberries	rosemary

How Much to Plant

Below you'll find a chart with average recommendations for how much to plant per person for a year's worth of food, and how much each plant produces on average. Keep in mind, these averages are based on good soil and may differ year to year. I find my tomatoes and beans produce much more than the average listed. Your actual yield will be affected by soil nutrition, weather, and pest conditions.

Dry Measurement Conversion by Volume

Bushel	Peck	Quart	Pint
4 pecks 8 gallons 32 quarts 64 pints 128 cups	8 quarts 16 pints 32 cups	2 pints 4 cups	2 cups

FRUIT	Plants per Person	Average Yield Per Plant
Apples		Dwarf: 5–6 bushels Semi-Dwarf: 10–15 bushels Standard: 5–20 bushels
Apricots		Miniature: 1–2 pecks Dwarf: 1–2 bushels Standard: 3–4 bushels
Blackberries	2–4 plants per person	35–70 cups per plant
Blueberries	2 plants per person	15–45 cups depending on maturity of plant
Cherries		**Sweet** Dwarf: 8–10 gallons Semi-Dwarf: 10–15 gallons Standard: 15–20 gallons **Sour** Dwarf: 3–5 gallons Semi-Dwarf: 12–18 gallons

FRUIT	Plants per Person	Average Yield Per Plant
Elderberries	1 plant per person	30-36 cups per mature plant
Grapes	1 vine per person	10-30 cups per vine
Nectarines		Miniature: 1–2 pecks Dwarf: 3–4 bushels Standard: 6–10 bushels
Peaches		Miniature: 1–2 pecks Dwarf: 3–4 bushels Standard: 6–10 bushels
Pears		Dwarf: 6–8 bushels Standard: 12–15 bushels
Plums		**European** Dwarf: 1–1½ bushels Standard: 1–2 bushels **Japanese** Dwarf: 3–4 bushels Semi-Dwarf: 4–5 bushels Standard: 5–6 bushels
Raspberries	10–25 plants per person	1–2 quarts per plant
Rhubarb	2–3 crowns per person	6 cups per crown
Strawberries	20–25 plants per person	1 pound or 1 pint per plant

VEGETABLE	Average Plants per Person	Average Pounds per Plant	Average Cups per Plant
Asparagus	10–15 per person average	2–3 pounds per plant	4–6 cups
Beans, Dry	15 plants per person	¼–½ pound per plant	2 cups
Beans, Snap	Bush: 15–20 plants per person Pole: 10–15 plants per person	½ pound per plant ½ pound per plant	Bush: 2 cups Pole: 3–4 cups
Beets	36–40 per person	¼ pound per beet	½ –¾ cup
Broccoli	3–5 plants per person	1 pound per plant	5–6 cups
Brussels Sprouts	2–3 plants per person	¾–1 pound per plant	4 cups
Cabbage	3–5 plants per person	2–4 pounds per plant	8–16 cups
Carrots	25–30 per person	¼ pound per carrot	¼ cup
Cauliflower	2–3 plants per person	2 pounds per plant	3–4 cups
Celery	3–5 per person	½ pound per plant	2 cups
Corn (Sweet, in husk)	15 plants per person	2 ears per plant	1½ cups

VEGETABLE	Average Plants per Person	Average Pounds per Plant	Average Cups per Plant
Cucumbers (3–5" pickling cukes)	2–4 plants per person	3–5 pounds per plant	8–15 cups (3–5 quarts whole)
Eggplant	1–2 plants per person	8–10 pounds per plant	32–40 cups
Garlic	15 bulbs per person		
Kale	5 plants per person	1 pound per plant	3–6 cups
Leeks	12–15 plants per person	¼ pound per plant	½ cup
Lettuces	5–10 per person	¼–1 pound per plant	4–6 cups
Okra	6–8 plants per person	1 pound per plant	1½ cups
Onions, storage	15 bulbs per person	½ pound	1 cup
Parsnips	10–12 per person	⅓ pound per plant	⅔ cup
Peas, field	30 plants per person	⅛–¼ pound per plant	¼ cup
Peppers	Hot: 1–2 plants per person Sweet: 3–4 plants per person	1–4 pounds per plant	3–10 cups

VEGETABLE	Average Plants per Person	Average Pounds per Plant	Average Cups per Plant
Potatoes	10–15 plants per person	2 pounds per plant	4 cups
Pumpkins	1–2 plants per person	4–10 pounds per plant	16–40 cups cubed
Rutabagas	5–10 plants per person	1–3 pounds per plant	1½–5 cups
Spinach	15 plants per person	¼ pound per plant	1½ cups
Squash, summer (pattypan, yellow, zucchini)	1–2 plants per person	5–20 pounds per plant	12–50 cups
Squash, winter (Hubbard, banana, acorn, butternut, buttercup)	1–2 plants per person	10–15 pounds per plant	10–15 cups
Sweet Potatoes	5 plants per person	2 pounds per plant	5 cups
Tomatoes	5 plants per person	5–15 pounds per plant	7½ cups–22½ cups
Turnips	5–10 plants per person	½ pound per plant	2 cups

GARDEN LAYOUT

Use these pages to sketch out how your garden area will look based on which plants you decide to grow to meet your family's food needs.

CONTAINER GARDENING

If your soil is clay or not in good shape, many people prefer to put in raised beds or to use large containers. This also works well if you don't have very much land. Even people with a back deck or small patio can do container gardening.

It's important to ensure that the container is large enough to support the root system of whatever you're planting. Make sure there are ample drain holes in the bottom of the container. You don't have to invest in fancy containers if you don't want to. Five-gallon food-safe buckets work well, and many times you can get them free from a local restaurant or bakery.

There are many container options available:

- plastic pots
- 5-gallon buckets (one of the easiest in both size and availability)
- grow bags (These come in sizes of 1, 2, 3, 5, 7, 10, 15, 20, 25, and 100 gallons. If storage is an issue, grow bags can be folded down during the off season. Remember, it is harder to remove and replace soil in the larger bags, so make sure large bags are in a permanent spot.)
- terra-cotta or clay pots
- glazed clay pots
- metal or tin pots
- repurposed items (Get creative! Think old rubber boots, watering cans, sinks and tubs, storage bins, garbage cans, old wheelbarrows, pails—anything that will hold soil and can be given a few drainage holes.)

To create drainage holes, use a drill with a ¼-inch bit or up to a ⅜-inch or ⅝-inch size. For a small container, two drainage holes are fine. As you go up in size, increase the number of holes. For a large container like a half whiskey barrel, we use five holes. If soil falls through your holes (or to avoid them being plugged) you can use mesh or a coffee filter to keep dirt from falling through.

A container creates a different environment than in-ground gardening or raised beds, where normal gravitational pressure forces the water through the soil. In a container, when the water gets to the bottom of the soil, there is no more dry soil (as in the earth) for it to travel to. This means soil in a container will end up holding more water than soil in the ground, and it becomes saturated faster. That's why soil choice is important in containers. It's a common myth that putting a layer of gravel in the bottom of a container will help with drainage. It's actually the size of the soil and its absorption rate that affect your drainage; adding gravel or rocks to the bottom of the pot does nothing for the rate of time it takes the water to move through the soil, but it does take up pot space and give your roots less room.

Due to gravitational and matric potential, you don't want to use your regular garden soil for a container. Your soil needs good air-filled porosity and water-holding capacity (which refers to the air and water the soil holds after watering). The most common potting mixes use coarse sand, peat moss, sawdust, vermiculite, and perlite.

You can purchase potting mixes or even the individual ingredients to make your own. Pennsylvania State University recommends a homemade mixture of equal parts (about one gallon of each) sterilized loam soil, moist course sphagnum peat moss, followed by coarse sand, perlite, or vermiculite.

BUYING SEEDS

So, you've got your garden spot picked out, and you've figured out whether you need to amend your soil. Now it's time to pick your seeds! We only grow foods from heirloom seeds—some of those varieties being ones my family has saved for generations. But how can you ensure you're getting good quality heirloom seeds?

Before we discuss where to buy seeds, it's important to know the different types of seeds.

Types of Seeds

There is a lot of confusion about the terms *hybrid*, *heirloom*, and *genetically modified*. Here is a quick walk-through.

Heirloom Seeds

These are open-pollinated seeds from varieties that have been handed down for generations (most sources say they're heirloom if you can trace them back at least 50 years).

Heirloom seeds are my favorite of the three seed types. When they are planted, they produce the same plant with the same characteristics of the parent plant that you saved the seeds from. This assumes you saved your seeds correctly when it comes to plants that cross-pollinate or are self-pollinated.

Plants that tend to cross-pollinate—squash, for example—need special care to be sure they don't cross-pollinate. Using methods such as hand-pollinating or seed netting to keep them pure will ensure you don't get crosses that are different from the parent plant.

Hybrid Seeds

In the context of hybrid seeds, we're talking about hybrid seeds that you purchase in the store. So F1, the first generation hybrid. These seeds are created by companies or scientists in a lab, not a natural cross-pollination that happens with heirloom varieties.

It was about the 1940s when large seed companies started creating their own strains of hybrid seeds. For example, two varieties of a tomato plant would be put together in a lab to create a different tomato plant. But this lab work is not a natural cross-pollination as we get with heirloom plants.

These hybrid seeds are created by combining two varieties of the same plant where the best characteristics from each variety are chosen to create a new hybrid plant. One may be more disease resistant, and the other offers a higher yield, and so on.

There's nothing wrong with hybrid seeds, but you're not able to save seeds from them, and there are fewer varieties to choose from.

GMO Seeds

The next type of seed (and this is where a lot of confusion comes in) are GMO seeds. A lot of people think that genetically modified seeds and hybrid seeds are the same thing and that we have had GMO seeds for hundreds of years. This is just not true.

Let's dive into GMOs a little bit. Genetically modified organisms, or seeds, in this case, are not for sale at your local big-box store or from regular seed companies. That's not to say that the seeds you purchase might not have genetically modified elements, but they are not purposely genetically modified.

Many large farms that supply to grocery stores purchase GMO seeds, and they need to have certificates for which seeds are used. (We'll talk a little bit more later about how there's contamination with some of the crops you are getting at the store because of GMOs.)

Genetically modified seeds are seeds that are created in a lab by splicing or combining different organisms—which can be viruses, bacteria, or even animal DNA—to create a patented plant.

For example, there is a GMO corn that has genetic material from bacteria, *Bacillus thuringiensis*, that produces an endotoxin.[3] There is also GMO corn that is resistant to chemical pesticide, which means the crops can be sprayed with weed-killing pesticide, and due to gene altering, the crop plant won't die. Sadly, over ninety percent of domestic corn in the United States is genetically modified.[4] The most popular GMO crops are

---

3 C.W. Schmidt, "Natural Born Killers," Pub Med: National Center for Biotechnology Information, September 1998, https://pubmed.ncbi.nlm.nih.gov/9721262/.

4 "Recent Trends in GE Adoption," U.S. Department of Agriculture Economic Research Service September 14, 2022, https://www.ers.usda.gov/data-products/adoption-of-genetically -engineered-crops-in-the-u-s/recent-trends-in-ge-adoption/.

alfalfa, canola, corn, cotton, papaya, soybeans, summer squash, and sugar beets. Recently the United States approved a GMO apple as well.

While you aren't going to find GMO seeds on store shelves, you may find foods that have ingredients that are GMO, such as soybean or canola oil. If it's labeled non-GMO, which is what I look for personally, then it's been tested and sourced from a non-genetically-modified crop. Anything that falls in the "certified organic" category isn't tested as often or as stringently as the non-GMO label, but when they do test for it, if it does show GMO, then you can't have the organic certification.

The Safe Seed Pledge is a voluntary pledge made by seed companies to not buy, produce, or sell GMO seeds. If a seed company has signed the Safe Seed Pledge, it's a good bet they're a safe company to buy from.

The Safe Seed Pledge reads:

Agriculture and seeds provide the basis upon which our lives depend. We must protect this foundation as a safe and genetically stable source for future generations. For the benefit of all farmers, gardeners and consumers who want an alternative, we pledge that we do not knowingly buy or sell genetically engineered seeds or plants. The mechanical transfer of genetic material outside of natural reproductive methods and between genera, families or kingdoms, poses great biological risks as well as economic, political and cultural threats. We feel that genetically engineered varieties have been insufficiently tested prior to public release. More research and testing is necessary to further assess the potential risks of genetically engineered seeds.[5]

---

5 "Safe Seed Pledge," High Mowing Seeds, accessed March 6, 2023, https://www.highmowingseeds.com/safe-seed-pledge.

Some of the companies I purchase seeds from are:

- Baker Creek Heirloom Seeds
- Seed Savers Exchange
- Seeds for Generations
- Siskiyou Seeds
- Johnny's Seeds

One of my best tips is to find a seed company that is growing their own seed (not just repackaging them from a larger supplier) in conditions similar to your own. Siskiyou Seeds is a company that grows their crops in farms located in Oregon and Washington (I live in northern western Washington). Because our growing conditions are so similar, I find their seeds perform better in my garden.

Heirloom Vegetables

Of all the information I could share about gardening, my greatest desire is to tell people about using and growing heirloom plants. The vastness of variety and flavor is beyond anything you're used to finding on your grocery store shelf or in the small set of hybrid seed packets for sale in many stores. They're the only seed you can save every year and have it grow back.

> Heirloom seeds are exactly as God created them when He made the world. They haven't been touched by scientists or manipulated like store-bought hybrid seeds, which are sterile, or like genetically modified seeds, which I believe can cause much harm to your health and to our natural ecosystem.

When my husband and I were first dating, he came to my parents' house for dinner. We'd been dating long enough that I knew he didn't like green beans. But it was his first time having a meal at my parents' home. It was summertime, and my mother had cooked up a big pot of our Tarheel green beans. When I saw him dish up some of the beans, I knew he didn't want to offend my mother by not eating what she'd prepared.

When my mother got up to get dessert, he

reached for the pot of green beans. I thought he was really trying to impress my parents. I whispered, "I know you don't like green beans. It's okay; you don't have to take seconds. My mom won't care."

He plopped a large spoonful on his plate. "I don't like green beans, but I love these."

Every spring of our marriage we have planted and grown these beans. My children won't eat green beans from the store or in a restaurant. They can taste the difference. So can I.

I've never found our variety of green beans in the store or seed catalogs. I've had people contact me over the years who haven't saved their seed and are eagerly seeking them out, or who have heard of the beans and want to try them. I'm sure my grandparents never imagined the reach this seed would have when they packed it with them.

PLANTING

It's time to plant! Putting the seeds in the garden is one of my favorite things. That simple action holds such promise and hope and reminds me of how God plants little seeds in our lives that later grow into full-fledged beautiful blessings.

There are two ways to plant your garden, depending on what you want to plant. One is to use transplants or seedlings, and the other is direct sowing. Direct sowing is simply putting the seed into the ground. Transplants and seedlings can either be purchased from a nursery or local gardening store or

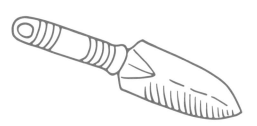

grown and nurtured from seed inside your home.

Transplants and seedlings can extend the growing season for those of us living in an area with a shorter or cooler summer. Tomatoes and peppers are two plants I must either start indoors or purchase seedlings for. You can even transplant sweet corn and snap peas to give you a thicker stand and a jump on the season.

You'll also see seedlings for most winter and summer squash. We typically wait to direct sow until the last part of May. Our growing season for warm-weather plants ends in September. This barely gives us four months.

I have grown seedlings for winter and summer squash, but I have found direct sown seeds to perform better. No matter how much care you use when transplanting the seedlings, it takes them a while to recover from the transplant and really start growing. The plants I've direct sown grow just as quickly as the transplants and many times outgrow them due to not having to recover from the transplant. Some plants, like beans, don't respond to being transplanted at all and should always be direct sown.

The success of your plants and harvest depends on putting your seeds or transplants into the ground at the right time. To do this, you need to know your area's average first and last frost date. You'll want to avoid putting out seedlings and the seeds of warm-weather plants until all danger of frost has passed. Vegetables that can be planted during the cooler months are spinach, lettuce, carrots, beets, cabbage, kale, broccoli, snow peas, and brussels sprouts. All types of squash, green beans, peppers, corn, and tomatoes require warm soil (over 65 degrees) and need to be planted after all danger of frost. To find your area's average first and last frost dates, you can do a simple Internet search or ask an experienced gardener in your area. Many local or independent nurseries also have this information.

Following is a full list of how early to start seedlings indoors and a chart of which plants to direct sow and when. Write in your sow date after researching the dates of your first and last frost. (When the "start indoors" column is left blank, this indicates that the plants will, generally speaking, perform better when direct sown.)

Plant	Start Indoors	Plant Outside	My Sow Date
Beans—pole and bush		3–4 weeks after last spring frost	
Beans, shellies or dry		3–4 weeks after last spring frost	
Beets		2-4 weeks before last spring frost or 4 weeks before first fall frost	
Broccoli	7 weeks before last spring frost	2 weeks before last spring frost	
Cabbage	6 weeks before last spring frost	2 weeks before last spring frost, or direct sow in mid to late summer for a fall crop	
Carrots		2-4 weeks before last spring frost. Can continue to sow up until 8 weeks before first fall frost.	
Cauliflower	8–10 weeks before last frost	2 weeks before last spring frost	
Chard	4 weeks before last spring frost	On last spring frost date or 6-12 weeks before first fall frost	
Corn		2-4 weeks after last spring frost	
Cucumbers	On last spring frost date	3-4 weeks after last spring frost	
Garlic		6-8 weeks before first fall frost	
Kale		4-6 weeks before last spring frost or 2-3 weeks before first fall frost	
Lettuce		4 weeks before last spring frost. Sow every 2-3 weeks for continual harvest.	
Onions	10–16 weeks before last spring frost	6 weeks before to 4 weeks after last spring frost	

Plant	Start Indoors	Plant Outside	My Sow Date
Parsnips		2 weeks before last spring frost	
Peas	8 weeks before last spring frost	4-6 weeks before last spring frost	
Peppers	4–8 weeks before last spring frost (8 weeks for cooler climates)	3-4 weeks after last spring frost	
Potatoes		2-4 weeks before last spring frost to as late as 2-3 weeks after last spring frost	
Rutabaga		4-6 weeks before last spring frost	
Spinach		6 weeks before last spring frost or 8 weeks before first fall frost	
Squash, summer	2 weeks before last spring frost	2-4 weeks after last spring frost	
Squash, winter pumpkin	2 weeks before last spring frost	2-4 weeks after last spring frost	
Tomatoes	2–8 weeks before last spring frost		
Turnips		2-4 weeks before last spring frost	
Watermelon	On last spring frost date	4 weeks after last spring frost	

In order to speed up the germination time (the time between planting the seed and seeing it sprout), we soak some of our seeds the night before planting. This helps shorten the germination time by at least a few days. I've had much higher success rates with my beet and bean seeds by soaking them. Just place them in a bowl of room temperature water overnight. In the morning, drain and plant your seeds. I don't soak tiny seeds, like tomatoes, peppers, carrots, lettuce, or spinach. Primarily, we just soak the beet, bean, and corn seed.

Check the forecast during planting week as you don't want to put your seeds in the ground if a huge rainstorm is on its way. One, it can wash the seed away if the rain is really heavy, and two, if the ground is too saturated, the seeds may rot.

When planting your garden, use the height of your plants to your advantage. Tomatoes, peppers, beans, and corn prefer full sun. Lettuce, spinach, and snow peas can tolerate cooler temperatures. Our beans are a pole bean, so they get to be about four feet tall. I'll plant our lettuce on the back side of taller plants so the plants don't get the full force of the midday sun. On the other hand, you wouldn't want to plant your corn in the front of the garden where it would keep all of the plants in the shade.

Six Tips for Planting Beans

1. **Direct sow your beans.** Beans do not grow well as seedlings or transplants. They are best sowed directly into the ground as a seed. Beans should be sown when the soil temperature (not the air temperature) is at least 60 degrees Fahrenheit.

2. **Soak your beans overnight.** The night before you plant your beans, soak the seeds overnight in room-temperature water. This will greatly speed up the germination process. However, if the weatherman foretells rain for your region during your bean-planting week, don't soak the seeds because they could rot.

3. **Plant your beans where your *Brassicas* were planted the previous year.** Beans are an excellent plant when it comes to crop rotation because they help fix nitrogen in the soil. It's a good idea to plant them

where *Brassicas* (like cabbage, broccoli, brussels sprouts, or cauliflower) were planted the previous year.

4. **Take advantage of companion planting.** Beans are a fairly non-picky plant and get along nicely with almost everything else. The only plants you shouldn't plant in their vicinity are members of the allium family, like onions, garlic, leek, and scallions. The allium family can inhibit or stunt the growth of green beans.

5. **Run a string over your planted bean seeds.** Birds are notorious for pulling up new bean sprouts. If you tie a string just an inch or two over the row of sprouts, it prevents the birds from pulling them up. After the beans are a few inches tall, you can remove the string.

6. **Know if the beans are a bush or pole variety.** The seed package should tell you this. Bush beans don't need a support system and are rather bushy and lower to the ground. Pole beans send up vine runners and need something to climb. You can use a pole, fencing, or even run strands of string or wire between two poles to create a trellis system. Once the runners begin to grow, you need to give the plants something to climb. They won't grow if they don't have their support system. After putting your climbing supports in place, the beans literally grow inches overnight. Our bean is a pole variety and quite prolific.

Six Steps for Successful Potatoes

1. **Only plant seed potatoes.** Potatoes you've purchased in the grocery store are not suitable for seed potatoes because they haven't been harvested that way. They also may have been sprayed with chemicals to keep them from sprouting on the shelf. Seed potatoes are chosen for their resistance to disease. I know some people do plant potatoes they've purchased from the store once they've sprouted, but I'd rather not take the gamble of introducing any disease to my soil.

2. **Choose acidic soil that drains well and has been fertilized.** Potatoes are heavy feeders. You don't want them to rot in the ground or develop

a fungus. Never plant where you had tomatoes, peppers, or eggplant the previous year. Always rotate your potatoes each year.

3. **Potatoes prefer cooler weather,** and they can be put in the ground as early as two weeks before your last frost date. They'll tolerate some heat, but if temperatures stay in the 90s or above for prolonged periods of time, they may die.

4. **Dig a trench about 4 to 6 inches deep.** Set the cut potato inside with the eye facing upward. Space the potatoes 12 inches apart and cover them with 2 inches of soil. After the potatoes have sprouted, you'll need to mound soil around them.

5. **Know your variety and when to mound your potato plants.** Potatoes are produced from the tubers, and if left exposed to light, they'll turn green and poisonous. (Yes, this is true.) Indeterminate potatoes should be mounded to increase the number of potatoes produced and to help inhibit blight. Use a hoe to mound the soil up around the plant once the foliage has reached about 8 inches high. It's better to not mound the soil too steep, so it won't wash away in the rain. Mound the soil until only 2 to 3 inches of leaves are left showing.

6. **Additional mounding of dirt should be done** once you have new growth of about 4 to 6 inches. This will be repeated 3 to 4 times throughout the growing season. If you don't have the garden space for potatoes, they make an excellent container crop. Instead of mounding, you simply fill the container with more dirt as needed. I've seen pictures of people using large plastic laundry baskets!

THE DIFFERENCE BETWEEN INDETERMINATE AND DETERMINATE PLANTS

Determinate varieties produce tubers (the potatoes) in a single layer, therefore they don't require mounding, and they have a shorter growing window. Indeterminate varieties will grow multiple layers of tubers (potatoes) and therefore you need to mound soil around the plants so the additional layers of tubers will form underground in the soil.

Growing Tomatoes 101

In the next chapter, I'll share with you about my troubled tomato-growing past. But here, I want to share what I learned about planting tomatoes. You know, just in case you struggle with them too.

Tomatoes prefer warm climates and don't like it when the night temperature drops below 50°F (10°C). They also start to fail to set fruit in temperatures above 95°F (35°C). They like a pH between 5.5 to 7.5, but the ideal pH is 6.0 to 6.8. Choose a warm, sheltered site with good airflow and 10 or more hours of daily sun.

The germination temperature is 60-90°F (16-32°C), but ideally 75-85°F (24-29° C). They should germinate in 5 to 14 days. Start tomato plants inside 6 to 8 weeks before your last frost date and plant them outside 2 weeks after your last frost date. When you plant them outside, make sure the soil is at least 60°F (16°C) and overnight lows aren't dipping beneath 50°F (10°C). It

---

TWO WAYS TO ADD CALCIUM TO SOIL

If your soil shows low calcium levels (a soil test is best to determine your levels) here's how to increase it:

1. **Eggshells:** At the time of planting, add ground eggshells to the planting hole. Grind up the eggshells very finely. For adequately fertile soil, you generally need 2 pounds per 100 square feet.

2. **Limestone:** If your soil is acidic, adding limestone (either calcium carbonate lime or dolomitic lime) can increase the alkalinity as well as calcium levels of the soil. If you already have high magnesium levels, do not add dolomitic limestone. For adequately fertile soil, add 6 pounds of limestone (in either form) per 100 square feet if the soil is claylike; add 4 pounds if the soil is loamy; add 2 pounds if the soil is sandy.

If you don't have slightly acidic soil to begin with, eggshells may not break down enough to provide extra calcium to your tomatoes. If you use eggshells, it's best to powder them in a coffee grinder or spice grinder or, alternatively, soak them in vinegar, let them dry, and then crush them up and put them in the soil.

is easiest to set up a support system or cages for the plants when you first plant them outside, to avoid damaging the plant later. If you live in a very long and warm growing season, you can direct sow seeds ¼ to ½ inch deep every 2 weeks for a staggered tomato harvest (succession sowing).

Tomatoes are heavy feeders and benefit from some preplanting amendments. Phosphorus is the most important nutrient for tomatoes. Incorporate compost into the top 2 inches of soil and then put a handful of colloidal phosphate (rock phosphate) or bone meal directly into each planting hole. High nitrogen fertilizer is helpful when the plants are growing quickly, but once the flowers appear, they need phosphorus more than nitrogen. (If you see a lot of foliar growth but not very many blossoms, it can be a sign of too much nitrogen.)

Tomatoes have specific soil needs. They can be prone to root rot, so a well-draining, loamy, moisture retentive soil is best. Tomatoes like a soil pH of 6.0 to 6.8 and need calcium to combat blossom end rot. Oftentimes calcium levels are sufficient in the soil, but blossom end rot will occur due to inadequate watering, which inhibits the plants from properly drawing up the available calcium properly. If your soil is poor, you can give your plants a foliar feed of compost tea or liquid kelp (fish fertilizer) every week until they start to flower. Then feed them every 2 to 3 weeks.

Go deep. Plant tomatoes all the way up to their first set of leaves to encourage a large root system for a healthier plant. You'll see small hairs on the stem of your tomato plant, and those hairs will turn into roots if they are covered with soil. The larger your root system, the more food and nutrients your tomato plant can take in, which will provide you with more tomatoes in return.

Water requirements for tomatoes are less than other plants. They don't need excessive water and too much will result in more and larger—but less tasty—fruit. Less water means smaller but tastier fruit. It is best to water deeply twice a week once the plants are established. Water at ground level and avoid getting water on the leaves as it can invite the spread of disease. Don't wait until you see signs of water stress as this can lead to blossom end rot (typically a result of uneven watering). Uneven watering can also cause fruit to split.

Common Pests and Diseases
There are a lot of enemies to the tomato plant. The potential pests include:

aphids	leafhoppers	tomato hornworms
cutworms	mites	slugs and snails
Colorado beetles	nematodes	
flea beetles	stink bugs	

The diseases that tomatoes are vulnerable to are:

anthracnose	blossom end rot	fusarium wilt
bacterial canker	early blight	verticillium wilt
bacterial spot	southern bacterial wilt	

You can keep some of these problems under control by rotation, by watering at ground level, and by not planting tomatoes where eggplant, peppers, or potatoes have grown in the last three years.

Diseases can be spread via wet leaves. Tobacco mosaic is also a serious disease spread by smokers who handle the plant after smoking cigarettes. Late blight is also something to consider, which is worse in cool, humid weather, in which spots appear on the leaves and then the whole plant turns black and dies, sometimes overnight. You may be able to control the spread of blight if you remove the plant immediately.

Companion planting is another good way to naturally deter pests from your tomatoes. For a full, in-depth look at companion planting, refer to my book *The Family Garden Plan*. Tomatoes and basil not only taste fabulous together, but they grow well together too. Basil helps to repel flies, and when it is grown near tomatoes, many think it increases their flavor. Another companion plant for tomatoes is calendula. Calendula deters worms and is a favorite of mine to use in homemade skin care products.

If you've ever tried growing tomatoes in a rainy climate, you know that rain increases the risk of blight and once a plant is infected, blight can quickly wipe out an entire crop. We can't stop the rain, but we do have a way to stop the rain from soaking everything.

Enter the basic functions of an umbrella. An umbrella was exactly what my tomatoes got! We had an old metal carport frame. The plastic tarp roof had long since rotted and ripped. But a good frame can be transformed into many a useful thing.

I purchased greenhouse plastic and fasteners and repurposed it into one big tomato umbrella (or cold frame, whichever name you prefer). While frost still kissed the ground, I started my tomato seeds indoors. Every day I'd carefully water them and rotate them underneath the grow light.

When it came time to set my darlings outside in the cold frame, I took two weeks to harden off my plants. (If you have a plant that's always been kept indoors, you have to gradually let it acclimate and build up a tolerance to the conditions outdoors. The first day you let it sit outside for an hour and then bring it back in. Each day you lengthen the time it is outdoors by an hour or two until you've reached a full 24 hours. If you don't take this time, your plant will most likely die from shock.)

I wound soaker hoses beneath the base of the plants. Not one drop of water was allowed to touch the leaves and tops of my plants. Tomatoes like to be watered deeply but less frequently, so instead of daily watering, I turned the hose on twice a week.

CROP ROTATION

After your garden is up and you can identify the plants by their leaves, take a picture. Next year when you go to plant, the photo will help you remember where everything was located. Trust me—your memory might not be quite as sharp as you think when you try to recall exactly where everything was a year later. The picture will prove invaluable and help you plot out your crop rotation.

Crop rotation is simply planting your plants in a different spot from the previous year. Different plants take different amounts of nutrients from the

soil. Rotating them by plant family and by whether the harvested portion is from the roots, leaves, or flowers will help keep your soil balanced and reduce the threat of insects and disease. By practicing crop rotation, you will reduce your risk of many soil-borne viruses and other soil problems that can negatively affect your plants.

There are two plant families that especially require crop rotation: Solanaceae and *Brassicas*.

The Solanaceae family includes nightshade plants like tomatoes, peppers, and potatoes. These are all susceptible to the same pests and diseases. You don't want to plant these in the same spot or soil where any related plants have grown in the past three years. Therefore it is also important to purchase certified seed potatoes when planting, as you can unknowingly introduce viruses to your soil otherwise.

The *Brassica* genus, sometimes referred to as cruciferous vegetables, includes broccoli, cabbage, brussels sprouts, and cauliflower. *Brassicas* like nitrogen-rich soil. Legumes (beans and peas) will put nitrogen back into your soil through their roots, so planting *Brassicas* where you had beans or peas the year prior is a good idea. As with the Solanaceae vegetables, don't plant *Brassicas* in a space where related plants have grown in the previous three years.

WEEDS

Let's talk about weeds. There are many different trains of thought when it comes to weeds in the garden. Some weeds are in fact edible, but you want to make sure you have a really good reference manual before pulling up and eating something without knowing exactly what it is, or what side effects it might cause.

There are basically two methods of weed control in the vegetable garden. I say two because we don't use chemical pesticides as a manner of weed control on our food, and I don't recommend it for anyone else. So it's either pull them up or suppress them. There are advantages to both methods, and you'll have to experiment and decide which works best for you and your garden, or incorporate them both.

Pulling Weeds

Manage weeds before they have time to take root in three steps.

1. Use stakes and string to lay out rows. Plant your seeds on a straight line and leave the string in place. (The string also keeps birds from pulling up your young seedlings.)
2. Water gently as necessary, avoiding too much cold water.
3. In seven to ten days, depending on the temperature, come back with a sharp (shallow is best) hoe and gently scrape or stir the top inch of soil around, avoiding the planted line. If you look carefully, you'll see the threadlike roots of emerging weed seeds, and you'll see that you've just killed most of the problem in less than five minutes. Timing is everything!

Of course, the most basic method is to simply pull up the weeds by hand when you see them. This takes time, and if you skip a few days—or a week or two—the weeds can quickly overtake your garden. We're normally fairly diligent, but this happened to us last year. While the weeds can steal nutrients from your

---

THREE WAYS TO ENJOY DANDELIONS

Dandelions are widely considered an annoying weed. However, dandelions can be harvested and all parts of the plant are edible. (Due to pollution, use caution when picking from anywhere the plants may have been sprayed or by busy roadways.)

1. The greens are best when picked young in the spring so they're not bitter. They can be steamed, added fresh to salads, or cooked in soups or casseroles.

2. Some people roast and grind up the roots for a coffee substitute.

3. I've also seen the blossoms dipped in batter and fried.

Dandelions have many vitamins and minerals and most of us walk over them every spring and summer, never thinking about a free food supply. We so often look at things as a nuisance or annoyance when really, they can be gifts. The changing of perspective is a wonderful thing. Instead of an annoying weed the dandelion may be your next culinary masterpiece . . . or at the very least a way to lower the cost of your food bill.

plants, if they are left to mature, they'll also go to seed and create even more weeds the following year. Another bad thing is we have poisonous nightshade that grows in our region. We discovered some of the weeds growing were nightshade berries. Yikes!

We donned gloves and pulled and bagged all the nightshade plants to avoid more reseeding. It was also a time to remind our kids to only pick berries and plants they knew were safe. I learned an important lesson: Stay on top of the weeds. Gardens always provide ample lessons, it seems. Avoiding your problems doesn't make them go away and usually only makes them worse.

If you dedicate 15 minutes a day to hoeing young weeds, you'll stay on top of them. While I can't put in an hour or even a half hour every day, I can always find 15 minutes. Make a plan to put in 15 minutes weeding every day and see how much you can get done. You may go over that, but if you do just the 15 minutes, you'll have accomplished quite a bit when you add it up at the end of the week.

If you've let your weeds go and need a restart, rototill between your rows to put the weeds back into the soil and knock them down. Of course, if you wait until they're going to seed, you're simply replanting more weeds. Rototilling can also cause compaction of soil, bring more seeds to the surface of the soil, destroy natural soil structure, and disrupt fungi growth. While tilling is not always bad, your soil will be healthier if you do so minimally.

Suppressing Weeds

Over the years, I've come to appreciate the suppression method for weed control above all else. Essentially, you're stopping them from growing in the first place, or drastically suppressing them. This is often referred to as no-till or lasagna gardening.

When you look at nature, you never see bare soil. Any time the soil is bare, after a fire for example, it will quickly begin to fill in with vegetation. Instead of fighting to keep neat rows of bare soil between your vegetables and flowers (which is a never-ending battle), use suppression to keep weeds to a minimum and enhance the health of your soil with mulch. Here are a few of the benefits of using mulch in the garden:

- Less soil erosion
- Better water retention and less overall watering
- More plant protection
- Weed suppression
- An improved food web (worm habitat) under the soil
- Added organic matter and nutrients
- Better soil temperature control
- Reduced overall waste

Mulch Options

- Straw
- Hay (may introduce additional weed seed)
- Shredded leaves (thick layers of whole leaves can block water and air and aren't advised)
- Wood chips (green chips are best)
- Lawn clippings (that haven't gone to seed yet)

It's important to note that when I'm using mulch, I'm still planting and growing in the soil. Pull back the mulch layer to get to bare soil when putting in starts, direct sowing seed, or applying any type of soil amendment. Once the seed has germinated and is a few inches taller than your mulch, you can spread the mulch up to its base, but not touching the plant. You want space for moisture to reach the roots and for the plant to breathe.

Straw and Hay

When using straw, inspect the bales and refuse any that have lots of seed heads (again, we're not wanting to introduce more seeds). In my experience and climate, hay molds too quickly and introduces new weed seeds to the area. With straw or hay, you want to ensure that the fields were not sprayed with herbicides that negatively impact vegetables.

It's common for straw and hay to be sprayed with a class of herbicides known as pyridine carboxylic acids. Vegetables are affected by this class, especially tomatoes, peppers, beans, and peas (Solanaceae and legume families). The past few years, many home gardeners have reported using straw and losing their tomatoes shortly after applying it as mulch. I don't share this with you to scare you, just to make you aware and help you have conversations with the farmers you're purchasing your hay and straw from.

Straw and hay should be applied three to six inches deep. Straw helps with moisture retention, a huge benefit in hot months or dry climates. Straw and hay will break down faster than wood chips and will need to be reapplied once or twice a year.

Wood Chips

Wood mulch is what we now use for most of our gardens. In fact, wood chips provide every one of those potential benefits in that earlier list. Just to keep your gardening learning curve interesting, I should tell you that there is more than one kind of wood chip. There is always more to know about everything.

Arborist wood chips are made from all parts of the tree: leaves, branches, bark, and trunk. Usually, it is from freshly pruned or removed trees (fresh and still green). This is ideal, as there are more nutrients available, and as they break down, the wood chips will feed your soil. You can sign up on sites like chipdrop.com to have them delivered to your home (waiting times vary).

> Use caution if using all wood as your mulch that you're only using it on top of the soil (don't mix it in). If you incorporate undecomposed wood into your garden soil, it will bind up nitrogen for a period and may result in poor growth of vegetables. However, as long as the wood chips are left as a top dressing only, depletion is negligible.

Shredded wood mulch is usually from the bark and trunk of the tree. My husband works at a sawmill, and we have access to this. It's finer, which can result in clumping, and it breaks down faster. It works wonderful for weed suppression, but there isn't any green material (leaves) and the wood has been down for a while, so it doesn't offer as many nutrients for the soil as the arborist wood chips. However, many lumbermills will give it away for free or allow you to purchase it in bulk, which is cheaper than buying it by the bag at stores.

Bagged wood mulch is something you can buy in large plastic bags at nurseries and garden departments. It's hard to determine the age of these wood chips and it's usually more expensive than the other options.

The only type of wood chips you should avoid are those from black walnut trees, as they contain a biochemical called Juglone. This chemical is toxic to many plants and is best avoided. Cedar wood mulch and chips are fine to use.

Whatever you use, wood chips are best applied after direct sowing or transplanting small seedlings. Apply chips two to four inches deep. With the exception of blueberry plants, don't girdle the trunk of trees if using wood chips, make sure they're pulled back from the trunk by a few inches.

The mulching method, if done correctly, prevents weeds in two ways. First, it smothers existing weeds so they don't have enough light to grow. Second, it provides a protective layer so seeds from new weeds can't reach the soil and take root.

We use the second method in the fall on our garden in the form of either a cover crop or a thick layer of leaves. Instead of leaving our soil bare through the fall and winter months, we place a thick layer of fallen leaves over the dirt. This helps keep it from eroding away during the heavy rains or snow and also keeps any seeds blowing in the wind or from birds flying overhead from being "planted" into our soil. Finally, it provides beneficial nutrients to our garden as it breaks down and is eventually tilled back into the soil come spring.

You can do the same thing with a cover crop. We've used kale as a cover crop, but many popular choices are annual rye grass, buckwheat, and clover. Cover crops should be sown about four to six weeks before your first hard frost.

Regardless of the mulch method you choose, you will need to reapply it as it breaks down, and even when done to the appropriate depth, you will still have some weeds come up. The good news is, there will be drastically fewer weeds, and they will pull up much easier than those in non-mulched areas.

Lawn Clippings

The opportunity to have lawn clippings as a mulch resource is a good reason to have a lawn mower with a catcher. As you mow your lawn, you are generating a great weed-free, high nitrogen, easily handled fertilizer and mulch. Lay it one to three inches deep (depending on how big your plants are and how much lawn you have) alongside your berries and vegetables as they grow. If you leave it in piles, it will start cooking and melt, so you need to distribute it as you generate it or within a day or so of mowing.

THIRSTY PLANTS

You've done it. You've decided where to plant, gotten your soil ready, and put in your seedlings. Now what?

You'll want to make sure your garden stays well-watered, but not overly so. Soil that drains well will keep plants from drying out too quickly or becoming waterlogged and rotting. Even in the rainy Northwest, we still have to water in the latter part of summer. If you use the mulching method of weed control, you won't have to water as often, as the mulch will help keep the moisture in the ground and stop it from evaporating as quickly.

You may wish to use sprinklers, but use care with tomatoes and peppers when watering overhead. Overhead watering with tomatoes can introduce fungus and split the ripe tomatoes. Truly, the best practice is to use drip hoses, or to water by hand. However, if you have a large garden, watering by hand is going to be too time-consuming. I recommend investing in some soaker hoses.

Soaker hoses are porous and weep water, rather than having water come out the end or spray like a sprinkler system. These are wonderful for areas where mildew or fungus are a problem, as they only wet the ground and not the foliage. Because the water comes out slowly, there tends to be less runoff and the ground and roots of the plant get a better soaking (hence the name) than with the use of traditional sprinklers or over-head watering systems. They also use less water. One caveat: Don't turn your water on full-force or you can blow out the hose. Keep the pressure down. You can also bury the soaker hoses, but we keep ours above-ground since we move our tomatoes and peppers every year.

The time of day to water is also up for discussion. Never water during the hottest part of the day. You'll shock your plants, plus a lot of the water will evaporate before soaking into the dirt. Some gardeners like to water in the evening since the moisture will stick around longer as the sun won't be up for hours. However, this can introduce mildew or fungus when the water sits on the plants longer. Other folks prefer to water in the early morning. Your schedule will also determine when you water. If you leave extremely early in the morning, going outside to water the garden will most likely not happen.

Decide what works best for you and your region. I prefer to water in the morning when I can, but there are times I have to switch it around and water at night. Since we started using the soaker hoses, it doesn't matter as much in regard to morning or evening, since the foliage of our plants aren't being sprayed. We've also had fewer problems with mold and mildew on our plants.

PEST CONTROL

We need to talk a little bit about pest control. Some plants are more naturally inclined to attract and harbor pests than others. Tomatoes are often susceptible to disease, and worms and moths like to bother broccoli. In the southern states, squash is bothered by vine borers. Here, we battle with deer who find our garden as tasty as we do.

As with humans, a healthy plant will be more likely to withstand an invasion and come through it alive. So keep plants healthy with well-prepared soil and proper watering.

Our best protection from deer is good fencing. A good guard dog will also help. (Ours is not. He seems to think the deer make a lovely addition to the landscape.)

Several insects love all members of the cabbage family (*Brassicas*). The best remedy seems to be floating row covers that will keep them from getting to the plants in the first place. A word about row covers: In addition to keeping bugs away from most crops, they hold more heat around the plants. This is especially helpful in the spring or fall when the nights get cold. Row covers can help young seedlings get established and offer protection from the wind. They also keep crows from stealing newly emerging peas and corn.

I have also used organic neem oil on our potatoes and tomatoes during a flea beetle infestation. Our fruit trees were plagued by a small black aphid, and I used a treatment of neem oil for them as well. Even with organic methods, make sure to wear proper protective gear, such as long sleeves, pants, gloves, and a mask when applying treatments. Whenever you're spraying, make sure there's no rain in the forecast, and spray in the morning when there's less chance of a breeze.

TEN TIPS FOR PEST CONTROL

1. **Healthy plants are less susceptible to diseases and pests.** Start with well amended soil by the addition of compost and cover crops. And remember, pig, chicken, llama, horse, and cow manure are all excellent sources of natural organic fertilizer when allowed to properly age.

2. **Crop rotation.** Practicing crop rotation will cut down on many soil-borne viruses and diseases, saving you a lot of angst and time in the garden.

3. **Monitor your garden regularly.** An early detection of a pest or disease problem will often be the key to successfully eradicating it.

4. **Manually remove certain pests.** Some pests are easiest to remove by hand. When we had an infestation of flea beetles on our tomato plants, I manually removed them every morning and evening for a week. Spray aphids with a strong stream of water to dislodge them from plants.

5. **Bring in good bugs.** Another way to get rid of aphids is with ladybugs, which can be purchased at garden stores. Let the good bugs take care of the bad bugs.

6. **Diatomaceous earth (DE).** Purchase food grade DE when using it on edibles and in your vegetable garden. DE is a white powder made from the crushed-up fossilized remains of phytoplankton. When sprinkled on ants, fleas, and mites, it compromises their exoskeletons. It's safe for humans. You can use it to clean chicken coops and to help get rid of mites in your coop. DE is great for beans, broccoli, and cabbage to keep the bugs from crossing the soil to get to the plant. To apply, sprinkle it on the soil surrounding the plant. It's also a much better solution for slugs than salt. Salt kills slugs, but it also damages your soil.

7. **Organic neem oil (from the African neem tree).** It's best to spray your plants early in the morning. Never spray your plants in the heat of the day (when you could scorch or burn the leaves), at night (when the dew could wash the spray off), or before rain. You should also be careful not to apply it on a windy day; you don't want the spray getting in your face or skin. Neem oil requires two applications about 10 days apart. Be sure to label your spray bottle. Don't save the spray; use it all at once and mix a fresh batch for each application. Anytime you're applying a substance to your plants, use proper safety measures and caution.

8. **Row covers or cloth covers.** For plants that don't require cross-pollination by bees, using a row or cloth cover in the early spring will keep moths from laying their eggs in the plants.

9. **Netting and fencing.** Huge pests to our garden and plants are deer, elk, birds, and occasionally cattle when they wander out of the pasture. Our free-range chickens can also pose a problem to our fruit and vegetable crop. We use netting and fencing to keep the larger pests away. Plastic netting works great on blueberries and raised beds. We protect our garden with metal T-posts and metal fencing. Our young fruit trees have four tall metal T-posts around them, and we use chicken wire and plastic fencing around the main part of the tree and fruit.

10. **Watering.** Be sure to check your water levels. If the plant is stressed from lack of water, any kind of pest will kill it that much faster. A deep watering once or twice a week is much better than daily watering. Soaker hoses on the tomatoes and peppers overnight provides a much greater benefit than daily watering.

CHAPTER 2

HARVEST

The LORD will indeed give what is good,
and our land will yield its harvest.

PSALM 85:12

While there is a joy and a lesson to be learned during the planting of things, there is nothing as rewarding as your actual harvest. Plucking sunripened food straight from the vine is an experience everyone should have during their life.

The harvest is the reason we keep tending the garden, even when storms ravage and disease runs rampant. We slog through the mess and put in the work, knowing it will all be worth it in the end. The harvest is what will keep you returning to your garden year after year.

෨

There is little in life more rewarding than going out to your garden for your first harvest. All the work and planning are worth it when you get to eat something grown on your own land and from the fruits of your own labors. Your homegrown food will have more flavor as you harvest it at its peak time, allowing it to fully ripen on the vine and develop all of its flavor and nutrients.

While rewarding, harvest time can also feel overwhelming, as if everything is coming in at once. Another reason I recommend starting small! You might be surprised by how much you reap at the end of a season.

If you have more produce than you can deal with, consider giving some to family, friends, and even your local food bank. During the peak months of harvest in my area, July and August, there is usually always a bag or two of fresh garden produce in the foyer at church for the taking. Those are the good problems of a good harvest.

Another good problem? You will have gained a lot of knowledge about nature, how to work with plants and soil, what to try, and what to try later when you have more wisdom. You will know so much more about what grows in that container on the patio or what thrives in that patch of soil on the east end of your house. And you will definitely discover many things about your disposition as a gardener.

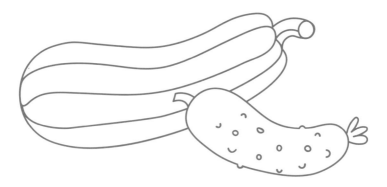

Have you ever noticed how most gardeners are willing to share their knowledge and advice? Get them talking about soil or strains of plants and you may think your feet are going to grow roots before the conversation is over. Well, you very well may become one of those people. I hope you do. I think the world would be a better place if we were all willing to share our knowledge. And we don't earn our right to share tips and tales unless we've first tried our hand at this thing called gardening.

When we're attentive and persevering gardeners, we will begin to harvest crops beyond our wildest dreams. I don't know about you, but I want buckets and bushels full of a godly harvest in my life and garden. And the very lovely, good problem of having an abundant harvest of nourishment and wisdom to share from!

AN ABUNDANT HARVEST

Squash and cucumbers

Some of the most prolific vegetables are summer squash. Cucumbers and zucchini can easily produce more than you're able to keep up with. In fact, one to two hills (containing three plants each) are more than enough for one family. When harvesting, be sure to lift the leaves of the plants, as cucumbers and zucchini will often hide under large leaves. It's best to check your plants daily during the peak of summer production.

> **ZUCCHINI ROUNDS**
>
> Another favorite zucchini treat is to slice them into thin rounds. Beat an egg, dip zucchini rounds into the beaten egg, drag them through seasoned flour or cornmeal, and bake them on a cookie sheet at 350°. Flip them over at 10 minutes and bake for another 10 minutes. Sprinkle grated cheese on top and bake for a final 2 minutes or until the cheese is melted.

Cucumbers are best when harvested small, especially for pickling. Small cucumbers make crunchier pickles. If cucumbers are smooth and turning yellow, they're generally overripe. Small zucchinis are favorable for grilling.

We slice ours lengthwise, rub them with a little bit of olive oil, sprinkle with salt, and grill for a wonderful side dish.

However, large zucchini can also be hollowed out and stuffed with meat and cheese. They can be grated for zucchini bread, cake, muffins, pizza crust, and as an addition to sauces. There's not much you can't sneak some grated zucchini into.

Garlic

We plant our garlic in the fall and harvest in mid-July. There are two kinds of garlic: soft-necked and hard-necked. Hard-necked garlic is ready to harvest when the top four to six leaves turn yellow and wither. Soft-necked garlic is ready to harvest when the stalks fall over.

To harvest garlic, use your hands or a shovel to loosen the bulb. If you use a shovel, be careful not to slice into the bulb. Pull up the bulb and knock off the largest of the dirt clods from the roots.

Garlic needs to cure before storing. To cure garlic, let it sit in a warm area with good ventilation for two weeks (more if it's extremely wet or humid). We thread our garlic through a square piece of wire fencing and hang it on our covered back porch. You don't want to let your garlic cure in direct sunlight. The sunlight can burn the garlic and reduce the flavor.

After garlic is cured, trim the roots and brush off the now-dried dirt. Don't remove more than a layer of the garlic's skin as this helps it keep a longer shelf life.

Soft-necked garlic can be braided and hung in your kitchen. Hard-necked garlic can be gathered together by its stalks and stored.

Onions

Onions are ready to harvest when their stalks begin to fall over, the same as garlic. Use the same techniques for harvesting. To cure onions, we put two large screens or wire on a sawhorse and place the onions on top. Let them sit in a dry, well-ventilated area to cure for two to three weeks.

Tomatoes

Tomatoes are one of the few fruits that can still ripen on the vine even after the vine is pulled from the soil. If you live in an area with a shorter growing season, you may have tomatoes still on the vine waiting to ripen at the end of the growing season.

If your tomatoes are not under cover and a big rainstorm is moving in or a frost is predicted, pull your tomatoes up, vine and all. Hang the plants in a dry, temperature-protected area where air can circulate. The tomatoes on the vine will continue to ripen over the next week or two, even though they're not in the ground.

Beans

If you're harvesting shelled beans (to use as a dried bean) or saving seeds from your beans for next year's planting, let the end of the garden season do the drying for you. If a rainstorm is moving in before you have time to shell the dried beans on the vine, or before they've fully dried, pull them up, plant and all, just like we do tomatoes. If they are not fully dried, hang them in a covered dry area. If they are fully dried, but you haven't had time to shell them yet, place them in a large bucket or container and move them to cover until you have time to shell them.

I've had mine in a bucket until close to Christmas before I got around to shelling them out. If there is any moisture on the vines or pod, though, they can start to mold, so you need to be sure they're dry and brittle if you're not going to shell them out quickly.

> There are four pecks in a bushel and each peck is two gallons, so that's eight gallons of tomatoes for a bushel.

GROWING A GARDENER

I promised to share the story of my tomato trail of tears. The good news is that it ends up being a tomato triumph. But it is important to understand that the path to being a proficient gardener can be a winding one. You will have wins and losses. And seasons where you might be tempted to think your labor was wasted. I'm here to tell you that the effort is not wasted at all.

By digging in to this endeavor, you are not only investing in growing a garden, you are investing in growing a gardener—you! Each season will provide information and wisdom that helps you the next season. May you be encouraged by my story. As you get to know other gardeners and swap stories, you will discover that almost every one of them has a garden nemesis—mine happens to be the tomato.

Some may respond to that with, "Tomatoes aren't hard to grow; they're super easy. All I do is plop mine in the dirt and I get tons of tomatoes all summer long. Aren't they the simplest plant to grow?"

Some folks have responded in this very way. And I, in turn, had to chew

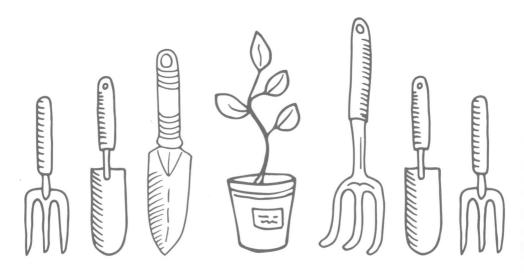

on my tongue. I do that when my first reply isn't gracious and kind. My tongue gets chewed on more than I care to admit. Every time I hear someone say tomatoes are one of the easiest plants to place in one's garden, my face heats up. My toes curl. My fingers clench into fists. Tomatoes are not one of the easiest plants to grow. In fact, they may be one of the hardest. I tried unsuccessfully for years to grow good large-crop producing tomatoes.

If you're one of the above people who have awesome luck with tomatoes, you're hereby required to share your tomato knowledge with the rest of us not-so-great tomato raisers. Or you can just bring us over a bushel of ripe tomatoes.

I had tried tomatoes in all different ways. I tried the hanging-upside-down method. I've grown them in raised beds and in pots. I've put them against our hot tub in the sunniest spot with the most southern exposure. I've placed them underneath the eaves of the house to keep the rainwater off them.

All to no avail.

The ones in pots never went beyond their blossoms. They had tons and tons of blossoms, but no fruit, despite my talking sweetly to them (alternated with a good stern if-you-know-what's-good-for-you warning). The ones hung upside down shriveled up and died. The ones under the eaves of the house developed large black spots of blight all over the fruit before it could ripen. And the ones that didn't develop blight just plain never ripened.

I became so frustrated by harvesting zero tomatoes that I took a year off from trying. A girl can only handle so many disappointments in a row. But after having to purchase bushels of tomatoes to can my salsa and stewed

> Ever cut into a tomato and had juice seep everywhere? When you make sauce or salsa, you want it on the thicker side, not a watery, soupy mess. Plant a paste tomato so the offerings have less water and thicker flesh. Both the San Marzano Lungo and the Amish Paste are wonderful.
>
> Can you use a non-paste tomato? Certainly, but the yield of your recipes won't be as high. The recipes will also take longer to make and won't be as flavorful.

tomatoes, the frugal side of me overrode the disappointed side. Patience is a virtue in one's spirit and life and in one's growth as a gardener.

I kept telling myself that thousands of people grew tomatoes every year. I would join their ranks. Some day.

I researched and collected all the tomato-growing tips I could find. I questioned people, read countless articles, and changed pretty much everything about the way I raised tomatoes. And despite all my prepping and planning, I anxiously awaited the first fruits. Clusters of blossoms dotted the vines. In the past, I had blossoms, but they never formed into tomatoes. I was almost afraid to hope. But I did.

My tomato plants dripped bright green tomatoes. Every day I ventured out into the greenhouse to check on their progress, diligently checking for signs of disease and removing any leaves that were discolored or shriveled.

One morning I walked into the greenhouse. Red tomatoes glistened on the vines like ornaments at Christmas. I may have wept just a little.

We harvested bucket upon bucket of tomatoes. Gorgeous vine-ripened, bursting-with-flavor tomatoes.

I rejoiced in those tomatoes. We had fried green tomatoes, tomato salsa, and pico de gallo, and the preserving of the harvest began. For years I've wanted to make and can my own tomato sauce, but I never had enough. You need quite a few tomatoes to make a decent-size batch of sauce, as in 35 pounds. I waited and waited for there to be enough ripe tomatoes at once. By the way, I learned that you can pick the tomatoes as they ripen. Simply freeze them until you have enough to make a batch of sauce. Thaw, and the skins will slip right off, then process into sauce. With my 18 tomato plants, I didn't have to use this method, because I had plenty of them ripe at once.

Homemade tomato sauce has so much more flavor than sauce from the store. I was amazed at how sweet it tastes all on its own. After dishing up our first spaghetti made with my homemade sauce, my husband said, "This is the best I've ever tasted."

We've successfully grown enough tomatoes to provide all of our family's

tomato needs for the entire year for six years straight (with the exception of ketchup, I do still buy ketchup from the store). All of our tomato sauce, salsa, stewed tomatoes, and dehydrated tomatoes that fill our pantry are from our garden.

And with all that tomatoey goodness, the greatest harvest of all has been the patience, perseverance, and practical wisdom I've gathered and been able to share with others. Finally.

REAP THE REWARDS OF A PLAN

Make a plan for your coming harvest. Remember to go simple and small in the beginning. You will gain confidence with each successful harvesttime. And, as my life clearly shows you, you will also gain a lot of valuable information if you happen to experience a less-than-successful harvest.

The following charts will help to set you up for the best possible outcome. They also become a quick-reference for you each year. With added notes from your experience or garden journal entries, you'll have annual records of what you need, what you've tried, and what you have reaped.

Plant	My Sow Date	Days to Harvest	My Harvest Date
Beans, pole and bush		60	
Beans, shellie or dry		85+	
Beets		50+	
Broccoli		80+	
Cabbage		70+	
Carrots		55+	
Cauliflower		50+	
Chard		50+	
Corn		60+	
Cucumbers		70+	
Garlic		9 months	
Kale		80+	
Lettuce		50+	
Onions		90+	
Parsnips		120+	
Peas		55+	
Peppers		50+ from planting outdoors	
Potatoes		90+	
Rutabaga		80+	
Spinach		40+	
Squash, summer		50+	
Squash, winter/ pumpkin		90+	
Tomatoes		80+	
Turnips		40+	
Watermelon		70+	

Be sure to also record how many plants you've sown (for example, two twelve-foot rows, three hills of five plants each) and your eventual crop yield (50 pints canned, 20 cups frozen, and so on). Keeping detailed charts of all this information will be invaluable as you plan next year's harvest!

The chart below will help you for harvesting and preserving.

HARVEST AND PRESERVING CHART

Crop	Harvest Tips	Fresh Volume	Canned	Frozen	Preserving Methods
Apples	Fruit will separate from the branch with an easy twist when ready.	1 bushel (42–48 pounds)	12–16 quarts	28–36 pints	Can, dehydrate root cellar, ferment, freeze
		3 pounds	1 quart	2 pints	
Apricots	Harvest when fruit is yellowish-orange and slightly soft to touch—don't allow to get mushy or overripe.	1 bushel (50 pounds)	20–25 quarts	40–50 pints	Can, dehydrate, freeze
		16 pounds	7 quarts	14 pints	
Asparagus	Harvest in spring when spears are 8 inches tall, snap off at soil line.	3–4 pounds	1 quart	3 pints	Can, dehydrate, ferment, freeze
Beans, dry (shelled)	Harvest when pods are swollen and lumpy; you'll feel the mature bean inside	5 pounds	7 quarts	14 pints	Can, dehydrate
Beans, snap (green bush or pole)	Harvest when pods are about 4–7 inches (length dependent on variety) and when pod is smooth (not filled out or lumpy with the bean inside) and crisp when snapped.	1 bushel (30 pounds)	15–20 quarts	30–45 pints	Can, dehydrate, ferment, freeze
		1½–2 pounds	1 quart	2 pints	

Crop	Harvest Tips	Fresh Volume	Canned	Frozen	Preserving Methods
Beets	Best harvested when 2½ inches or smaller in diameter. If soil is soft, grasp greens at the base and pull; if compacted, dig roots up. Hold beet in one hand and greens in the other, twist to break off the greens (leave about an inch of top stem to prevent bleeding).	3 pounds	1 quart	2 pints	Can, dehydrate, root cellar, ferment
Berries, general (except strawberries)	After color change, gently tug on the berry; it should pull free easily. If not, it's not quite ripe yet.	24–quart crate	12–18 quarts	32–36 pints	Can, dehydrate, freeze
		5–8 cups	1 quart	2–3 pints	
Blackberries	Gently tug on berry, it should easily come off, if it holds, wait another day or two.	12 pounds	7 quarts	14 pints	Can, dehydrate, freeze
		1¾ pounds	1 quart	1 quart	
Blueberries	Wait until berries are blue and fall into your hand when touched, if you have to tug the berry loose wait a few more days.	12 pounds	7 quarts	14 pints	Can, dehydrate, freeze
		1¾ pounds	1 quart	1 quart	
Broccoli	Many sources say to harvest in morning while cool. Harvest when heads are firm, before they've begun to swell up or flowered.	1 bushel (23 pounds)		46 pints	Dehydrate, freeze
		1 pound		2 pints	

Crop	Harvest Tips	Fresh Volume	Canned	Frozen	Preserving Methods
Brussels Sprouts	Wait until the first frost for best (and sweetest) flavor. Use a sharp knife to cut sprouts from the stalk when they're firm and approximately 1½ to 2 inches in diameter.	1 quart (1 ½ pounds)	2 pints (may only can if pickled)	2 pints	Freeze, root cellar
Cabbage (fermented sauerkraut)	Harvest when heads are firm (size depends on variety). Take a knife and cut the head from the stalk at the base. You might get lucky and have a smaller head grow back if you leave plant in the ground.	25 pounds	9 quarts (can only can if first fermented as sauer-kraut)	9 quarts	Can (sauer-kraut), dehydrate, ferment, freeze, root cellar
Carrots	Pull up from tops; if soil is hard/compacted, loosen with a garden fork first. Trim tops an inch from carrot.	½ bushel (25 pounds)	10 quarts	16-20 pints	Can, dehydrate, ferment, freeze, root cellar
		2-3 pounds	1 quart	2 pints	
Cauliflower	Cut when heads are tight and compact.	2 medium heads	2 pints (may only can if pickled)	2 pints	Can (pickle), dehydrate, freeze

Crop	Harvest Tips	Fresh Volume	Canned	Frozen	Preserving Methods
Celery	Harvest individual stalks from the outside of the plant when they are big enough to your liking (a minimum of 6 inches on outer stalks from the ground to the first set of leaves). Harvest whole plants by cutting at the soil line. Can survive light frost if covered.	1 plant (7–9 stalks)		1 pint	Can (only in tested combination recipes), dehydrate, ferment, freeze
Cherries	Fully colored and still firm to touch; taste test.	1 quart (2–2½ pounds)	1 quart, unpitted	1 quart, unpitted	Can, deydrate, freeze
Citrus	Citrus doesn't ripen off the tree; taste test before picking.	5–8 lemons = 1 cup juice 8–12 limes = 1 cup juice 2–4 oranges = 1 cup juice	Can grapefruit and oranges whole; other citrus may be used in combination canning recipes	You may freeze citrus whole to use later for zest and juice	Can, dehydrate, freeze, salt preserve
Corn, sweet (in husk)	Silk turns brown. Pierce an inner kernel partway down the cob; if juice is milky or white, it's ready. To pick, pull down and twist to break off the stem.	1 bushel 48 ears, (35 pounds) 6–16 ears	8–10 quarts 1 quart	14–17 pints 2 pints	Can, dehydrate, ferment, freeze

Crop	Harvest Tips	Fresh Volume	Canned	Frozen	Preserving Methods
Cranberry	Two types of harvest: dry and wet. Dry harvest is used primarily for cooking and baking. Wet is used for juices, sauces, and dried.	12 pounds	7 quarts	14 pints	Can, dehydrate, ferment, freeze
Cucumber	Slicing cucumbers are best around 6 inches in length. Burpless cucumbers should be 1½ inches in diameter. Cut or twist off from vine.	1 pound	1 quart (whole pickles)		Can, dehydrate, ferment
Cucumbers (3–5" pickling cukes)	Harvest pickling cucumbers between 3 to 5 inches long, when ridges and bumps are present.	1 bushel (48 pounds)	24 quarts	48 pints	Can, dehydrate, ferment
		8 pounds	3 to 4 quarts	7–9 pints	
Dates	Harvest when brown and wrinkled.	1 pound		2 ½ cups pitted	Dehydrate, freeze
Eggplant	Harvest when skin is thin and glossy and eggplant is firm to the touch and is large enough size to eat.	1 bushel (33–35 pounds)			Can (pickle), dehydrate, freeze
		1 pound	2 pints (only if pickled)	4 cups diced	

Crop	Harvest Tips	Fresh Volume	Canned	Frozen	Preserving Methods
Garlic	Harvest approximately 9 months after a fall planting on a dry day. Hardneck garlic is ready when the top three sets of stalks start to brown, softneck is ready when stalks fall over. To pick, loosen dirt with a garden fork and pull up from base of the stalk or dig up. Cure for storage.	12 pounds	5 quarts or 10 pints pickled garlic		Can (pickle), dehydrate, ferment, root cellar
Grapes	Sweeter after a frost. Harvest on a dry day, if possible, for extended shelf life. Grapes do not ripen off the vine; taste test before picking.	1 bushel (44–50 pounds with stems)	16 quarts of juice		Can, dehydrate, freeze
		2 pounds	1 quart (whole grapes)	1 quart	
Greens	Harvest when leaves are between 4 to 8 inches long (older or larger will taste bitter).	1 bushel (18 pounds)	6–9 quarts	8–12 pints	Can, dehydrate, freeze
		3–4 pounds	1 quart	2 pints	
Kale	Harvest when leaves are large enough. Increased flavor after a frost.	4 pounds	1 quart	2 pints	Can, dehydrate, freeze
Leeks	Harvest when stalks are 1 inch across.	2 large (1¼ pound)			Dehydrate

Crop	Harvest Tips	Fresh Volume	Canned	Frozen	Preserving Methods
Lettuce	Harvest leaf varieties when leaves are between 4 to 8 inches long (older or larger will taste bitter).	⅓ pound per head			May dehydrate into a green powder
Nectarines	Ready when skin turns color but fruit is still firm to the touch.	11 pounds	4 quarts	9 pints	Can, dehydrate, freeze
		2½ pounds	1 quart	2 pints	
Okra	Harvest when pods are 2 to 3 inches long. Wear gloves and cut stem above cap with a knife.	1 bushel (26–30 pounds)	17 quarts	34 pints	Can, dehydrate, ferment, freeze
		1½ pounds	1 quart	3¾ cups frozen	
Onions, storage	Harvest when stalks fall over on a dry day. Use a garden fork to loosen dirt (careful not to pierce the onion) and pull from base of stalk. Cure for long-term storage.	2 pounds		2 pints	Can (in combination recipes or pickles/ relishes), dehydrate, ferment, root cellar
Parsnip	Best flavor after hard frost. May leave in ground to overwinter. Loosen soil with garden fork and harvest.	1 bushel (50 pounds)	25 quarts	50 pints	Dehydrate, freeze, root cellar
		1 pound (4 medium or 5–6 small)	1 pint	1 pint	
Pea, field	Harvest peas when pods are swollen and you can see/feel the formed pea inside.	1 bushel (30 pounds)	6–7 quarts	12–15 pints	Can, dehydrate, freeze
		4–5 pounds	1 quart	2 pints	

Crop	Harvest Tips	Fresh Volume	Canned	Frozen	Preserving Methods
Pea, sugar snap	For sugar snap or whole pod eating, pick when pea is slender and young. For shelled peas, wait until pod is swollen and lumpy; shell out mature peas.	1 pound		2 pints	Freeze
Peaches	Ready when changes color and slightly soft to touch.	1 bushel (48 pounds)	18–24 quarts	32–48 pints	Can, dehydrate, freeze
		2–2½ pounds	1 quart	2 pints	
Pears	Must be picked early. Pears don't ripen on the tree. Waiting until completely ripe before harvest gives a hard, gritty flesh and the core will rot because they ripen from the inside out.	1 bushel (56 pounds)	20–25 quarts	40–50 pints	Can, dehydrate, freeze
		2–2½ pounds	1 quart	2 pints	
Peppers, hot	May harvest while still green, but both sweet and hot peppers will have more flavor (and spice on hot varieties) when allowed to mature and change color. Twist off at the stem or use a knife.	2 pounds	4 pints	4 pints (⅔ pound = 1 pint frozen)	Can, dehydrate, ferment, freeze

Crop	Harvest Tips	Fresh Volume	Canned	Frozen	Preserving Methods
Peppers, sweet	May harvest while still green, but both sweet and hot peppers will have more flavor when allowed to mature and change color. Twist off at the stem or use a knife.	9 pounds	9 pints (canning for pints only)	9 pints	Can, dehydrate, ferment, freeze
Plums	Harvest when skin color has darkened, are soft, and come off the tree with a slight twisting motion.	1 bushel	24–30 quarts		Can, dehydrate, freeze
		2–2½ pounds	1 quart	2 pints	
Potatoes	May harvest young "new" potatoes by pulling the plant or feeling around in the soil to select harvest and leave the plant. For a mature main crop, wait until the plant dies back and don't water two weeks prior to harvest. Use a broad or garden fork to loosen soil. If you leave some behind, you'll find them in the spring when you're digging up the garden to plant again.	1 bushel (60 pounds)	42 quarts	84 pints	Can, dehydrate, root cellar, freeze
		10 pounds	7 quarts, cubed	14 pints	
Pumpkins	Ready when stem has started to dry and skin begins to harden. For orange varieties, color change from green to orange is another indicator.	one 10-pound pumpkin	4 quarts	9 pints	Can, dehydrate, freeze, root cellar

Crop	Harvest Tips	Fresh Volume	Canned	Frozen	Preserving Methods
Rhubarb	Harvest when stalks are 10 to 15 inches long in the spring.	1½ pounds	1 quart	4½ cups	Can, dehydrate, freeze
Rutabagas	After a couple hard frosts, pull or dig them up and cut the tops an inch from top of root.	1 bushel (56 pounds)	23 quarts	56 pints	Can, dehydrate, freeze, root cellar
		1 pound	1 pint	2⅔ cups diced	
Squash, summer (pattypan, yellow, zucchini)	Pick when oblong (zucchini) squash are approximately 8 to 12 inches long. For pattypan or circular shaped squash, pick when 4 to 8 inches big. Check daily, summer squash grow extremely fast. Twist at the stem to remove it from the vine.	1 bushel (40 pounds)	Only can in pickled/relish form	26 pints	Can (pickle), ferment, dehydrate, freeze
		1½ pounds		1 pint	
Squash, winter (Hubbard, banana, acorn, butternut, buttercup)	Ready when stem has started to dry and skin starts to harden.	1 bushel (40 pounds)	16–20 quarts	32–40 pints	Can, dehydrate, freeze, root cellar
		3 pounds	1 quart	2 pints	
Straw- berries	Harvest when berries are fully red.	24-quart crate	12–16 quarts	38 pints	Can, dehydrate, freeze
		6–8 cups	1 quart	2 pints	
Sweet potatoes	Ready when large enough to harvest or vines/leaves start turning yellow.	½ bushel (25 pounds)	10 quarts	20 pints	Can, dehydrate, freeze, root cellar
		2–3 pounds	1 quart	2 pints	

Crop	Harvest Tips	Fresh Volume	Canned	Frozen	Preserving Methods
Tomatoes	Pick when skin yields slightly to finger pressure or has changed from green to variety color. Note: shoulders are the last part to change color. They will ripen off the vine but best flavor is vine ripened.	1 bushel (53 pounds)	15–20 pints or 10–12 quarts juice	15 pints	Can, dehydrate, ferment, freeze, root cellar for unripe green tomatoes
		2½–3 pounds	1 quart canned	2 pints	
Turnips	Harvest when turnips are 2 to 3 inches in diameter (or younger for the greens).	1 bushel 50 pounds	25 quarts	50 pints	Root cellar
		1 pound	1 pint	1 pint	

CHAPTER 3

PRESERVE

Blessed is the one who perseveres under trial because,
having stood the test, that person will receive the crown of life that
God has promised to those who love him.

JAMES 1:12

Preserving food is one of my favorite pioneer tasks. There is little that is more satisfying than gazing at stores of food you grew and preserved yourself. I have a slight addiction to Mason jars and have been known to gaze at jars of home-canned goods like one would a fine piece of art.

Even if you can't grow it at home, knowing how to preserve food when it's in season for use throughout the year is one of the most frugal and rewarding things you can do. While there are certain safety factors one needs to adhere to with home food preservation, it is an old-time tradition every home should learn and practice.

෨

I come from a long line of home food preservers. I grew up to the hiss and jiggle of my mother's pressure canner from midsummer through fall. The ping of canning lids ensured that we would have food for the winter. It's still one of my favorite sounds. Seriously, I have the urge to fist pump when I hear those pings.

When my husband and I first got married, our favorite Christmas gift was the box from his grandmother, packed with home-canned jars of pickles, popcorn balls, cookies, and strawberry jam.

Later, as I progressed in my canning experience, I attempted the strawberry jam. I ended up with delicious but unintentional syrup. It would not set! In a serious humble mode, I asked his grandmother for a lesson. And a priceless lesson I received: You can only make one batch at a time when using regular store-bought pectin. Even though it's the same ratio of ingredients, you cannot double a batch. It won't set.

Now, as long as I stick to the small-batch method, my pantry remains lined with a plethora of homemade jams and jellies. The only time I have syrup is if I set out to make it.

Home canning may seem like a lost art, but I'm seeing its resurgence, and I'm so glad. There are many reasons to learn this skill. Canned food is easy to store, and it's a meal source that stays safe even if there are power outages. Another reason is convenience. After a long day, just pop open a few jars of canned food and heat it, and you've got a from-scratch, home-cooked, wholesome meal on the table.

In the aftermath of COVID, we've seen how fragile our supply chain is. Not only does preserving your own food act as insurance against supply-chain breakdowns and pandemics, but food preserved at home allows you to control what goes into your food. It seems we're hit with another news update every week about a food recall or a new discovery on the dangers of substances allowed into our food by large companies.

Growing and preserving our own food has been one of the single biggest catalysts to increased health and a lower food budget. Children are great to show you things you say a lot. Whenever my daughter sees me get out my canning jars and canner she says, "Are we putting this up for winter?"

It makes me smile every time. "Yes, we're putting this up for winter."

CHOOSING PRODUCE TO PRESERVE

If you're not able to grow everything at home, you can still save considerable amounts of money by putting food up yourself. By purchasing fruits and vegetables when they're in season, you're able to get them at a lower cost and higher quality. Many times, you can save even more money by purchasing those items in bulk or going to a u-pick farm.

If I don't grow enough of an item myself, I prefer to go to a u-pick farm or farmers' market. A u-pick farm is preferable because you can pick the produce when it's at its prime, not overripe or underripe. Though for jam making, if a portion of your fruit isn't at its ripest, it has a slightly higher level of natural pectin. It's recommended to use one-quarter underripe fruit in your jam recipes for a thicker set.

If none of those places are available, become good friends with the produce manager at your local grocery store. They can tell you when the new produce arrives and is freshest.

To take advantage of the low seasonal prices, you'll want to purchase enough of each item to see you through to the following year. This amount will vary for each family.

I don't purchase jam or jelly from the store—ever—so I know I need to make enough to last us until the next berry season. We grow our own raspberries, blueberries, blackberries, and strawberries. However, our strawberry plants don't provide us with enough berries for all the jam we can eat. We're lucky enough to have a u-pick farm a few miles up the road from us. I usually pick their organic strawberries twice during the season. We go through approximately two jars of jam a month, so I like to have two dozen jars (a mixture of different kinds) for the year, with extras to give out as Christmas gifts.

It's a good idea to keep track of what your family eats and goes through in a month and then average that out for the year. Here is a chart of the best times of the year to buy seasonal produce on average. Times for locally grown produce vary slightly by region.

Season	Fruits	Vegetables
January-February	Citrus fruits (oranges, lemons, grapefruit, tangerines), papaya	Broccoli, brussels sprouts, cabbage, cauliflower, kale, parsnips, turnips, potatoes
March-April	Mango, pineapple, rhubarb	Artichoke, asparagus, new potatoes, radishes, spring peas, snow peas
May-June	Apricots, rhubarb, strawberries	Lettuce, new potatoes, spring onion, swiss chard, zucchini
July-August	Blackberries, blueberries, boysenberries, cherries, melons, peaches, plums, raspberries	Corn, cucumbers, eggplant, garlic, green beans, lettuce, okra, onions, peppers (sweet and hot), summer squash, tomatillos, tomatoes
September-October	Apples, dates, figs, grapes, pears, pomegranates	Acorn squash, butternut squash, carrots, garlic, kale, onions, potatoes, pumpkin, spaghetti squash, spinach, winter squash, tomatoes
November-December	Apples, cranberries, dates, pears	Beets, brussels sprouts, cauliflower, carrots, celery, leeks, parsnips, potatoes, pumpkin, rutabaga, sweet potato, swiss chard, turnips, winter squash

CHOOSING YOUR PRESERVING METHODS

Once you purchase your produce you've got several options for preserving it. Of course, we like to eat some of it fresh, but the rest we preserve for year-round eating. The main methods of preserving fruits and vegetables are freezing, dehydrating, canning, fermenting, freeze drying, salt, and root cellar or cold storage techniques. Some herbs can also be preserved in alcohol to make your own tinctures and extracts.

When choosing which method of preserving you'll use, you need to consider how you want to later use the food. For example, if you prefer to use

Preserving Supplies Checklist

Canning (water bath)

- [ ] Large pot with lid or water bath canner with rack
- [ ] Canning rack (can use extra bands or twisted towel to keep jars up off the bottom of the pot)
- [ ] Canning jars, lids, and bands

Canning (pressure canning)

- [ ] Pressure canner with rack (you cannot can in an electric pressure cooker; must be a stove-top pressure canner)
- [ ] Canning jars, lids, and bands

    Canning supplies that are nice to have but not essential:
    - Jar lifter
    - Headspace measuring tool

Dehydrating

- [ ] Dehydrator and trays
- [ ] Mason jars or sealable, air-tight bags

    Dehydrating supplies that are nice to have but not essential:
    - Silicone nonstick mats or parchment paper for fruit puree, sticky fruit, or small pieces of food
    - Vacuum sealer, bags, and mason jar attachment

Freezing

- [ ] Freezer containers or bags
- [ ] Steamer basket to blanch some vegetables
- [ ] Mason jars make excellent freezer containers for many fruits (I freeze quart jars full of berries).

    Freezing supplies that are nice to have but not essential:
    - Vacuum sealer, bags, and Mason jar attachment

Fermenting

- [ ] Mason jars or fermenting crock
- [ ] Airlock system for jars
- [ ] Fermenting weight (you can use a plastic bag or small jar filled with water as a homemade weight)

Root Cellar

- [ ] Screen or wire to lay crops on during curing
- [ ] Breathable containers, bags, or bins to store cured vegetables in

zucchini in stir-fry or in quick breads, then freezing is probably your best option. For quick breads, I grate up my zucchini, squeeze out the excess moisture, and vacuum seal it in two-cup portions. For stir-fry or to add to stews and soups, I either slice it in rounds or dice it before freezing.

I usually use a couple of methods for each food depending upon how I'll be cooking or eating it later.

Freezing

Let's first talk freezing, as this is the method most people have had some experience with. You'll need a freezer and freezer containers, usually freezer bags. I've found our vacuum sealer allows me to get more food into our freezer and does a better job at keeping freezer burn away from the food, prolonging its shelf life. I can also use the vacuum sealer with my dehydrated items. If you plan on preserving or putting up a lot of your own food, you may wish to get one.

Berries lend themselves well to being frozen. Some people recommend flash-freezing them before storage—that is, laying them out in a single layer on a tray to freeze them before putting them in a bag. I don't bother with this. I pour raspberries, blueberries, and blackberries straight from my colander into my freezer bag and pop them in the freezer. They rarely stick together, and if they do, I can pull them apart quite easily with my fingers. The key to this is making sure they're not wet before freezing.

> If you don't have a vacuum sealer, freezer bags also work, but for long-term freezer storage, we've found a vacuum sealer has been invaluable.

Because I use organic methods at home and only purchase or pick organic berries, I don't soak or wash them before freezing. Unless, of course I happen to spill the whole bucket in the field! But I sample berries as I go. Nothing is as good as a sweet, ripe blueberry straight from the bush. I don't go in the house and wash it before I eat it. I don't see the need to do the same before I freeze them either. The one caveat to this is berries grown on the ground, like strawberries. They are low enough to the fertilizer used that there could be cross-contamination. Rinse them well, allow to dry fully, and then freeze. If you're unsure of the growing method, always rinse the berries.

You can also freeze berries you plan on making jam or jelly out of later. Usually when the berries are ripe, summer temperatures make you want to do anything other than heat up your kitchen with canning. Toss your berries into the freezer for a cooler day. Plus, frozen and then thawed berries give up their juice more easily, speeding up the cooking process. I also freeze my lemons and limes whole for this same reason when I need them for juicing and as my pectin source.

Some vegetables need to be blanched before being frozen. Blanching is the process of immersing the vegetable in either steam or boiling water for a short period of time and then immediately placing the hot food into cold water to stop the cooking process. The reason for this is to stop the enzymes from breaking down the food (causing decay), which will still happen even when frozen.

I tend to be a person who learns from mistakes instead of just following instructions. Something I'm working on. One year I decided to freeze some of our butternut squash and skipped the blanching step, thinking it was unnecessary. I peeled and cubed it and stuck it in the freezer. No matter how I prepared that frozen squash, it never tasted right. It didn't matter how long I cooked it, either—the texture was always a bit hard and woody. I ended up throwing most of it out.

The following year I took the time to prepare it correctly and it worked beautifully. It baked up exactly how fresh squash would, with perhaps a bit less cooking time. Lesson learned.

Below is a list of foods that can be blanched, as well as cooking times. Always wash and trim the vegetable before blanching as you would before cooking. For example, remove ends of beans, trim broccoli and cauliflower to bite-size pieces, peel and remove seeds from winter squash, and peel root vegetables.

BLANCHING TIMES FOR FREEZING VEGETABLES

Asparagus: Blanch in boiling water 2 minutes for small stalks, 3 minutes for medium stalks, and 4 minutes for large stalks.

Beans, green: Blanch in boiling water 3 minutes.

Beans, lima: Blanch in boiling water 2 minutes for small beans and 4 minutes for large beans.

Beets: Blanch until tender, then peel and chop to desired size. Blanch in boiling water 25 to 30 minutes for small pieces and 45 to 50 minutes for large pieces.

Broccoli: Most folks prefer steam-blanching rather than boiling. Steam for 5 minutes.

Brussels sprouts: Blanch in boiling water 3 minutes for small sprouts and 5 minutes for large sprouts.

Carrots: Blanch in boiling water 3 minutes for slices and 5 minutes for whole carrots.

Cauliflower: Blanch in boiling water 3 minutes.

Corn on the cob: Don't use overripe corn. Corn is at its peak and best for eating and preserving when it still has liquid inside the kernel. When pierced, the liquid should look milky. Blanch in boiling water 7 minutes for small ears, 9 minutes for medium ears, and 11 minutes for large ears.

Corn kernels: With the kernels still on the cob, blanch in boiling water 4 minutes. Allow to cool. Cut kernels off the cob and freeze.

Greens: Blanch in boiling water 2 minutes. After the ice-water bath, squeeze out excess moisture before freezing.

Peas: Blanch in boiling water 1½ minutes.

Rutabagas and turnips: Blanch in boiling water 2 minutes.

Summer squash: Blanch in boiling water 3 minutes.

Winter squash: Steam-blanch 20 minutes. I prefer to dice my butternut squash into ½-inch cubes. Acorn squash is usually mashed or puréed after blanching and then frozen.

When freezing any food, I find it works best if it's frozen in uniform pieces. All chopped up to roughly the same size. No need to bring out a measuring stick; just eyeball it. This way, when I'm thawing the food, it all thaws out evenly. Be sure to label your frozen food with the date and the amount. Practicing rotation in your pantry and freezer is key to using what you have and not having to throw out old food.

Fermenting

Fermenting is one of the oldest forms of food preservation but perhaps one of the least practiced in mainstream America—or maybe just not in the little town I grew up in. As a kid, I only knew one person who did any type of fermenting. Thankfully, this form of food preservation is making a comeback and since the first edition of this book, there are now whole sections at even major chain groceries stores with kombucha, water kefir, and kimchi.

The good news is, fermenting is extremely easy to do at home, and when you do it yourself, you'll save a lot of money. Fermenting food uses a culture of good bacteria and naturally occurring acid to preserve the food. This method contains many health benefits along with its preservation benefits. Fermenting vegetables (think sauerkraut, pickles, kimchi) is done by using a salt water brine and time.

This process is called lactic acid fermentation. Lactic acid is formed when naturally occurring yeast and bacteria convert sugars into lactic acid. This naturally preserves the food for long-term storage (as long as proper temperatures are maintained) and is the typical form used for fermented vegetables.

Fermenting is wonderful because you don't need anything other than a vessel (glass jar or

FOUR WAYS TO CHECK YOUR FERMENT

How do you know your ferment is fermenting? Here are the signs of fermentation action that we want to see happening:

1. Bubbles near the top
2. Cloudy brine
3. Duller colors (for example, it goes from bright green to a more army green)
4. Liquid level is still above the vegetables

TRADITIONAL SAUERKRAUT

Makes about 2 quarts

Ingredients:

1 head cabbage (purple or green)
1 T. sea salt

Directions:

Shred the cabbage, either using a knife or with a food processor.

Place the shredded cabbage in a large bowl, sprinkle salt over it, and mix it together. Let it sit for at least 30 minutes.

Stir the cabbage and let it sit for another 20 to 30 minutes, until you have enough juices to cover the cabbage when it is packed into your jar or fermenting vessel.

Transfer the cabbage to your container. A wide-mouthed mason jar in a quart or ½-gallon size works great.

Press down hard on the cabbage so the liquid rises to the top and covers the cabbage.

Place your fermenting weight on top to hold the cabbage down beneath the brine level.

Put your lid or airlock on top. If using a band, tighten it fully and then back it off a half turn, and make sure to burp your jar every day.

Allow the cabbage to ferment for 7 days, and then check for flavor. Depending on the temperature of your home and your preference, it may take anywhere from 1 to 4 weeks for the right flavor to develop.

After it's reached its desired flavor, remove the weight or airlock, and transfer the jar to cold storage (usually your fridge).

fermenting crock), vegetables, and your salt brine. Some vegetables require you to mix salt and water together in a specific amount (the level of salt is to prevent bad bacteria from growing until the good strains and lactic acid can develop), while others, like sauerkraut, simply use the salt and the liquid it pulls from the vegetable itself.

Fermented vegetables are probably one of the easiest forms of fermentation (and food preservation) you can start with. It's as simple as mixing some vegetables with salt water brine and letting them sit at room temperature anywhere from 3 days up to 2 or more weeks.

How long a specific ferment takes to finish is dependent on your taste preference and the ingredients used.

Something like sauerkraut can ferment for 2 to 4 weeks, the flavors will change throughout the entire process, and many times people will then move it to cold storage to sit for 6 or more months for the flavors to develop and mellow out a bit.

The best thing you can do is to experiment and find what you and your family like best. After all, that's the point of this from-scratch and homemade adventure: to make things you and your family like.

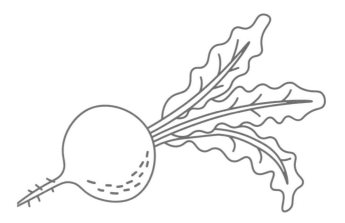

Fermenting Supplies

There are a few supplies to aid in your success when fermenting vegetables.

Fermenting weights: It's important that your veggies stay submerged below the brine. Food ferments in an anaerobic environment, meaning an environment without oxygen, so any food exposed to air will quickly mold and ruin the whole ferment.

Fermenting lid: I also like using something like a pickle piper lid, which is specifically designed to fit on a mason jar, but you can use a metal canning lid and band applied loosely and "burp" the jar (simply loosen the band to let any build-up of gasses escape) every day while the jar sits at room temperature.

Filtered water: When making fermented vegetables, it's important to try and use water that is as pure as possible. Any chlorine, fluoride, or other mysterious items found in tap water need to be avoided at all costs.

Pure sea salt: You'll also want to use pure sea salt. Avoid salt that has iodine added, as this will negatively affect the ferment. I use Redmond's Real Salt (I buy mine in bulk 25-pound bags).

Best Vegetables to Ferment

Many vegetables make wonderful ferments, but not all are used in the same way, and some aren't great candidates for fermentation due to their soft consistency.

Cabbage is wonderful shredded for sauerkraut, cucumbers are great fermented whole, while carrots are delicious when peeled, quartered lengthwise, and turned into fermented ginger carrot sticks. Here is my list of the best vegetables to ferment:

Beets	Garlic	Radishes
Cabbage	Jalapenos	Snap beans
Carrots	(and other peppers)	Tomatoes
Cauliflower	Kohlrabi	Turnips

Having not grown up with fermented food, my first few tries came from grocery stores. I knew it was good for me, but I wasn't really that impressed

BASIL SALT

Makes 6 ounces

You can substitute in any leafy herb; celery leaves are another favorite. If you'd like to do different or larger amounts, just keep the ratio of 4 parts fresh herb to 1 part salt.

Ingredients:

½ cup fresh basil leaves with stems   2 T. mineral salt

Directions:

Rinse the leaves and allow them to air-dry on an absorbent towel. Finely chop the herbs. Place the herbs and salt into a food processor and pulse until thoroughly combined. Put the herb-salt mixture into a glass jar with a lid and store it in the fridge for up to a year.

Use this in place of salt in any recipe. This is especially delightful in tomato soup or tomato sauce.

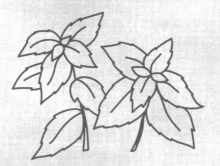

with the flavors. Like most things you make yourself, homemade simply tastes better, and ferments aren't any different.

I don't like store-bought sauerkraut, but homemade? I make multiple quarts, if not a gallon at a time. The intensity of the "fermented sour flavor" is determined by how long you let it ferment at room temperature. The warmer the room, the faster it will ferment. Depending on your taste buds, you may like the flavor after a few days while someone else likes it after ten days. Neither is wrong. Remember, when you move your ferment to cold storage (usually a fridge) it will continue to ferment and develop a stronger flavor, but it's MUCH slower than when at room temperature.

Dehydration

Dehydrating is another form of food preservation. Having an actual dehydrator will open up the possibilities of the kinds of foods you can dehydrate, including making your own powders from tomatoes, greens, and broth, to name a few. However, you can use your oven and the sun to dehydrate some foods.

Dehydration is simply pulling out the moisture from the food. Many people like dehydration for fruits, vegetables, and nuts because if done at a low temperature, the food still retains nearly all its vitamins and nutrients and is still considered raw.

The most frequently used dehydrated food in most homes is herbs. Those bottles of dried herbs you purchase at the grocery can be made easily at home and for a fraction of the price. I don't know about your grocery store, but some of those tiny bottles run upwards of six or seven dollars apiece.

Dried rosemary, dill, oregano, thyme, chives, peppermint, lemon balm, and sage are some of my favorite herbs to dehydrate. You'll notice basil is

Growing your own herbs is easy and something anyone can do. Southern-facing windows are excellent spots for a small herb garden indoors, and most herbs do quite well in containers on the porch or deck. Basil, rosemary, sage, and mint grow very well in containers. Mint and oregano will spread everywhere if not planted in a container to control them.

not among them. I find basil loses much of its flavor with dehydrating and is not worth the effort. Freeze-dried basil is just as pungent as fresh, but a freeze dryer is an investment piece of equipment and not one everyone has access to. Lucky for you, there's an easy, old-fashioned method of preserving basil that keeps it fresh for up to a year and retains ALL the flavor.

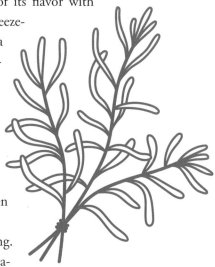

Herbed salts are one of my favorite ways to preserve basil and celery leaves (or any green leafy herb).

It's best to pick your herbs in the morning. This is when they have the highest concentration of oil in the leaves, which is where you get the flavor. Bring them indoors and rinse them if they're dusty. Spread them out on a clean, absorbent towel.

If you're using a dehydrator, lay them evenly on the trays. Remember, they'll shrink up considerably, so if you have the liquid liners for your dehydrator, use them to avoid letting the herbs slip through the cracks of the trays.

Don't have a dehydrator? Herbs are simple to dry without the aid of any appliances. When you pick them, leave them on the stem. Break the stem off at the base of the plant. Tie no more than five stems together (the air needs to be able to flow around and through them) and hang them upside-down in a warm area.

You don't want to hang them in direct sunlight. The sun can burn the leaves as they're drying. I use the rafters of the roof on our covered porch; some folks use the kitchen. I've also hung them near the chimney of our woodstove in the early spring when the sun was nowhere to be found and the outside air was a damp mess.

Check them every day or so. If you see any signs of mold or mildew on the leaves, discard them and move the herbs to a drier location.

Another option (especially if you live on a farm where there are flies and dust) is to place the herbs in a paper bag. Paper will allow air flow, but it will keep debris (and pooping flies) off your herbs. Don't pack the bag too tightly. I use a clothes pin to seal it shut and hang it from our back porch rafters. I've tried pillow cases in the past, but the herbs ended up molding in spots; the paper bag has worked better.

Depending upon the moisture content in the air, they're usually fully dry within a week. The leaves should be brittle and crumble when you rub them between your fingers. Place your dried herbs in a clean, dry glass jar. I use my smaller Mason jars or old spice jars. You can also find small glass jars with lids in stores or online. When not in use, store your herbs in a cool, dark cupboard.

Although you can simply use a knife to slice or chop all your foods for dehydrating, I've found a mandolin and a combination apple peeler and corer both make the job go much more quickly.

One of our favorite treats is dried apple slices. I put them through our peeler and corer, which also slices them into even ribbons at the same time. Some fruits, especially apples and pears, will turn brown once exposed to the air. You can avoid this by putting them in a lemon juice bath or dipping them in honey. Honey-dipped apple slices are great dehydrated (they will remain slightly tacky when dried), but our favorite—and quickest—treat is cinnamon apples.

CINNAMON APPLES

*Adjust your quantities based on how many apples you have on hand
and the space in your dehydrator.*

Ingredients:

apples
lemon juice and water bath (optional)
Ceylon cinnamon

Optional: nutmeg, ginger, and
sugar, to taste

Directions:

Prepare your apples by peeling, coring, and slicing them, then dipping them in a lemon juice bath if needed. Place the apples in a container with a lid or a large plastic bag, and add about a quarter cup of Ceylon cinnamon (if you want, add a few shakes of nutmeg or ginger for a slightly different flavor). Seal the container and shake it until the apple slices are evenly coated. You may add a pinch or two of sugar if your apples are tart. I prefer Honeycrisp, Gala, or Fuji apples, which are usually quite sweet on their own.

Evenly arrange the coated apple slices on your dehydrator trays so the apples aren't touching. It's important for the air to circulate freely around the fruit so they dry evenly. Set your dehydrator to its fruit setting (135°F). Check your fruit after a few hours. Drying time will vary depending upon how thick your fruit slices are. I rotate my trays once or twice during the drying process. You can't really dehydrate them too long. When the cinnamon apple slices are dry, transfer them to a clean, dry glass jar. I store mine in a quart-size Mason jar in the cupboard for several months.

NINE WAYS TO PRESERVE APPLES AT HOME

1. **Apple Pie Filling.** Is there anything better than lovely jars of home-canned apple pie filling? Yes, there is—diving headfirst into said jar with a spoon. Ever notice how apple prices go up during the holidays? You may can apple pie filling, or you may also freeze it. I peel, core, and slice up my apples, add my sugar and spices to the apples, place them in either a freezer bag and freeze them, or can them in quart-size Mason jars.

2. **Applesauce.** See instructions on page 106.

3. **Dehydrated Apples.** See instructions on page 97 and 98.

4. **Apple Scrap Cider Vinegar.** Yep, make your own lovely, fermented apple scrap cider vinegar. You won't believe how easy it is. Place cores and peelings in a clean Mason jar until it is approximately two-thirds full. Pour water over the top until the apple scraps are completely submerged. Cover the jar with a breathable towel or cheesecloth and secure it with a band. Allow the jar to sit for two weeks, stirring it once a day or so. Strain out the apple scraps and pour the liquid back into a clean Mason jar. Allow it to sit and ferment for another 2 to 4 weeks until it takes on a tangy vinegar smell.

5. **Apple Pectin.** You can make your own apple pectin by boiling apples (with the cores and peels) until they've turned mushy. Drain the cooked apples through cheese-cloth. Cook down the strained liquid until it's slightly thick, then freeze it and use it as pectin in all your homemade jams and jellies. Slightly underripe apples have higher pectin levels.

6. **Apple Butter.** Fruit butters are a delight and very easy to make.

7. **Apple Jelly.** I love apple jelly because all it takes is apple juice and sugar or honey. That's it, just two ingredients to make a delightful jelly to smear on pancakes, biscuits, waffles, toast, or to eat by the spoonful.

8. **Fruit Leather.** See instructions on page 100.

9. **Root cellar or cold storage.** Apples hold up well in a cool environment, and in proper conditions they will store clear through the winter. They prefer temperatures between 30 and 35 degrees with high humidity. However, don't let them freeze, or the cell walls will rupture and your apple, once thawed, won't be so yummy.

Fruit Leather

You can also make your own fruit leather at home. I think apple fruit leather is the easiest to make. You'll first make applesauce (see recipe on page 106), which is another staple on our homestead. For making fruit leather, allow the applesauce to cool until just warm so you don't burn yourself. I purchased silicone mats for my dehydrator for making fruit leather and drying sticky foods. Pour the applesauce onto the trays, spreading it out to an even thickness. Turn the dehydrator to 135 degrees and dry it until the applesauce resembles leather. Store it in a glass jar or airtight container. While it is warm, you can roll it up or just cut it into strips.

Pears also make a wonderful sauce and leather, so if you have an abundant pear crop or access to pears, you can use them in the same way.

Canning

If you've never canned anything before, I'd encourage you to start out with water-bath canning. Remember the jars of homemade jams and jellies your grandmother made? Those can be safely preserved in a hot pot of boiling water.

Canning Basics

Water-bath canning means processing your canned foods in boiling water for a specified amount of time. Acidic foods can safely be canned via the water-bath method (specifically foods with a pH level of 4.6 or lower). These are jellies, jams, preserves, marmalades, fruits, fruit spreads, fruit sauces, tomatoes (with acid added via lemon juice or vinegar), pickles, relishes, and chutneys. All you do is follow a tested recipe, immerse your filled jars in a bath of hot water with a canning rack, and boil them for the set amount of time.

Pressure canning heats your canned food under steam pressure, allowing for much higher temperatures and faster cooking times. All low-acid foods must be canned using a pressure canner. Low-acid foods include vegetables, meat, poultry, broth, and seafood.

In the past, people canned tomatoes using the water bath method without adding acid. However, tomatoes are borderline acidic, so to ensure safety, you should always add the specific amount of acid when canning tomato products to ensure a pH level of 4.6 or lower. Unfortunately, pH test strips are not accurate enough to use for testing your own canning recipes.

Wash your jars, lids, and bands in hot soapy water and rinse them well. You can keep your jars heated in hot water in your canner, but I keep mine in the hot wash water until I'm ready to fill them. Lids no longer need to be heated beforehand; boiling them or subjecting them to too much heat can actually damage the rubber on the lids and inhibit a good seal. (If you are water-bath canning for less than ten minutes of processing time, sterilize the jars by boiling them for ten minutes before you fill them.)

Fill your jars with your prepared recipe. If using the raw-pack method (not

> One of the benefits to pressure canning is you can raw-pack almost all your vegetables and fruits. It will cook fully while it's being canned.

precooking or heating the item to be canned), pack the fruit and vegetables into the jar and pour boiling water or syrup over the top. Don't fill the jars up to the very top; leave space between the food and the top of the jar (refer to chart below for the right amount of space). I prefer to use the raw-pack method for vegetables as it saves me time. Vegetables are fully cooked when they are pressure canned, so I see no reason to heat my kitchen up any more than necessary. Plus, I find I end up with crisper, less mushy vegetables using the raw pack method.

After filling the jars, remove air bubbles by sliding a knife between the side of the jar and your food. Run it around the inner edge of the jar.

Wipe the rim and threads of the jar with a damp, clean cloth. Place lids on the jars and screw the band down until resistance is met. Don't over-tighten, but make sure they're fingertip tight.

Type of Food	Amount of Headspace to Leave in the Jar
Fruit juices, pickles, jams, jellies	¼ inch
Fruits and tomatoes	½ inch
Vegetables, meat, poultry, seafood	1 inch

Fingertip tight is achieved by using three fingers (your thumb, pointer and middle finger) to tighten down the band. Once you feel resistance, go a quarter turn more. If you overtighten, you can cause lid buckling, which results in seal failure and non-shelf-stable jars.

When dealing with hot jars of food, I've found a jar lifter to be an invaluable kitchen tool. Oven mitts work in a pinch, but if they get wet, you can quickly burn a finger.

Place the jars in the canner, making sure the rack is in place. The rack keeps the jars from sitting directly on the heat source or the bottom of the pot. If the jars aren't on the rack, they can become too hot and burst or crack. If you don't have a rack, you can set the jars on old canning bands or even a folded-up towel, just so long as the jars are lifted up and the hot water can circulate beneath and around them. For water-bath canning, make sure the water covers the top of your jars by at least 1 inch. For pressure canning, follow the amount of water your manual suggests; mine calls for a quart and a half.

Put the lid on the pot during the water-bath canning process, and remove the lid when the processing time is complete, or as needed to check if the water is at a full boil. Start the time for your recipe when the water is at a full boil for water-bath canning or when the pressure control starts to jiggle. For pressure canning, you'll need to lock your lid into place, but don't put the pressure control on yet. Allow steam to come through the vent for ten minutes. This allows the pressure to build and ensures all of the air has been exhausted from both the canner and the jars of food. If air pockets are left, they can cause uneven heating during canning.

Pint-size jars hold two cups and quart jars hold four cups. Make sure your pressure canner holds both sizes so you only have to make one purchase.

Select the correct pounds of pressure for your food and put your controller in place. Once it begins to jiggle and hiss, at least three to four times per minute, start your timer.

SEVEN WAYS TO PRESERVE PUMPKIN

1. **Root cellar or cold storage.** Make sure the pumpkin is mature. The skin should be hard on the outside, and it's best if it's been allowed to mature on the vine. You always want to leave the stem on any squash you harvest, in order to preserve it longer. Pumpkins won't keep in cold storage as long as potatoes or other squashes, but they will be fine for two or three months. Be sure none of the skin of the pumpkin is punctured or blemished for this method. Wash the outside down and make sure it's thoroughly dry and has good air circulation. You can wipe the outside down with vinegar to help get rid of any bacteria that would make it break down faster. Pumpkins like temperatures between 50 and 55 degrees and 50 to 75 percent humidity.

2. **Cook your pumpkin.** There are two ways to cook pumpkin in order to use the following preserving methods. The method I've always used is to cut the pumpkin in half, scoop out the seeds, put it facedown in a roasting pan with about ½ to 1 inch of water, and bake it until it's soft. You can also put the whole pumpkin in the oven (provided it's not too big to fit) and roast it. Check it by inserting a knife, similar to how you'd check a baked potato, and allow the pumpkin to cool before opening it up.

3. **Freeze it.** You can freeze the roast pumpkin in cubes or purée. I usually put cubes of cooked pumpkin in a wide-mouth pint-sized Mason jar because most of my recipes call for 2 cups of pumpkin. It thaws really quickly and I purée it right before using in my recipes. You could put it in plastic freezer bags as well.

4. **Dehydrate it.** You can dehydrate pumpkin in either purée or cubed form.

5. **Pumpkin fruit leather**. Use pumpkin puree, applesauce, and spices and make a yummy fall fruit leather (see instructions on page 100).

6. **Pumpkin butter (NOT a canning option).** Pumpkin is low in acid and is only safe when pressure canned, but because pumpkin butter is thick, it's not safe to be canned in a pressure canner. Store-bought canned pumpkin items are done with industrial canners that reach much higher temperatures than home models. Homemade pumpkin butter is safe to freeze or store in the fridge.

7. **Canned cubed pumpkin (the only safe way to can pumpkin).** You may can cubes of pumpkin at home, but not pumpkin puree, butter, or pie filling. You put heated pumpkin cubes into the jar, pour heated cooking liquid over the cubes, and process in a pressure canner.

In the olden days, store-bought pectin was out of the question. I don't think my father's mother ever purchased it. My grandmother shared her knowledge and free pectin source. As you guessed, I'm about to do the same with you.

Pectin is a natural substance found in fruit—usually citrus fruits like lemons and limes. However, green or underripe apples, especially crab apples, also have a good amount of pectin in them (see page 99).

Another source of natural pectin can be found in currants (see recipe for Red Raspberry and Currant Jelly on page 110).

When time is up, allow the canner to cool according to the manufacturer's guide. When canning, this means allowing the canner to cool to air temperature on the stove over time. Never run a hot pressure canner under cool water to cool it down quickly.

Carefully remove the jars with either a jar lifter or an oven mitt. Set the warm jars on a double-folded towel. Allow the jars to cool for 24 hours without moving them.

After the jars are cool, test the lids for a seal. Press the center of the lid with your finger. It shouldn't flex. Remove the band and store the jar in a cool, dry, dark place, like a pantry shelf. The ultimate lid seal test is to remove the band (after the 24-hour cooling time) and lift the jar by just the lid. If a jar is sealed properly, the weight of the contents and jar will NOT cause it to unseal. If a jar isn't sealed, you have a 24 hour window to reprocess it. You'll need to use a new lid, bring the contents back up to temperature (bring jam back to a simmer, water to a boil when hot packing, etc.). If a jar doesn't seal, you can reprocess in the time frame or place it in the fridge to eat right away, or store it in the freezer.

Favorite Canning Recipes

On the following pages are some of my family's favorite canning recipes. You can find dozens more for whatever type of food you'd like to preserve, but make sure you're looking at a reputable source that follows up-to-date canning and food safety guidelines.

APPLESAUCE

Makes about 4 quarts

My favorite apples for applesauce are Gravensteins. The tree's twisted, gnarled branches reach out, and when laden with their green and blush of pink, it reminds me of how the garden of Eden must have looked. They're an old-fashioned heirloom apple. My parents have an old Gravenstein tree on their property that produces a bumper crop every few years. On those years, I make up as much applesauce as possible. The flavor is so perfect on its own; I don't add any spices or sugar. If you can get yourself some Gravensteins, grab them up; they're harder to find. We planted one in our orchard several years ago, but the trees take several years before they produce a good-size crop.

I usually choose seconds (apples of lesser quality) for applesauce. While I like a crisp apple for munching on, mealy or softer apples work great for applesauce and the method prevents them from going to waste, as most people don't like to snack on them.

Ingredients:

> **12 pounds of apples**   ¼ **cup lemon juice**
> **water**   **Optional: sugar, cinnamon, and nutmeg**

Directions:

The prep work on your apples will depend upon the equipment you have in your kitchen. If you have a sieve (conical shaped with small holes to catch the seeds and skins but allow the cooked food to pass through) or a food mill, then simply put whole apples into a large stockpot one to two layers deep. Add an inch or two of water (you don't want the water to cover the apples, as it would water down the finished sauce too much). With the lid on, bring the water to a slow simmer. Check your apples at 10 minutes for doneness and water level. You don't want to let the pot boil dry. You can stir the apples around a bit at this point to help prevent the bottom layer from scorching. Apples are done when the skins are split and they're soft all the way through.

When they're still warm, but not hot enough to burn you, run the apples through your sieve or food mill. Put the processed apples back into your stockpot. Use the skins to make homemade vinegar, feed them to the chickens (warning, chickens are very fond of apple scraps), or place them in your compost pile.

If you don't have a sieve or food mill, you'll need to peel, core, and slice your apples before cooking them (so go buy one immediately!). Put the apples in a large stockpot about ⅔ of the way full (with enough room to stir) and add a cup of water to prevent sticking. Bring them to a boil and allow the apples to simmer. Stir frequently to prevent scorching on the bottom. Once they are soft and cooked through, mash them with a potato masher.

When the apples have been sieved or mashed, heat the applesauce on medium until it's heated all the way through but not boiling. I generally do not add sugar to my homemade applesauce, but this will depend upon your variety of apples and palate. If I'm using a tart apple or they're a tad underripe, I add the smallest amount of sugar possible. I also like to add cinnamon and a dash of nutmeg. Add the lemon juice in and stir. The addition of lemon juice is to ensure the proper level of acidity.

I leave my jars in the hot wash water until right before filling them. Rinse the jars with hot water and place them on a towel folded over in thirds. Pour warm applesauce into the jars with a ½-inch headspace. Wipe the rim of each jar with a clean cloth and place lids and bands on the jars.

I put up both pint- and quart-size jars. The size you choose will depend upon the size of your family and how much you'll eat in one sitting. If I know I'll be doing a lot of baking, I open a quart-size jar. If it's just for snacking, I use the pint-size jar.

Applesauce is acidic enough that it can be safely canned in a water bath. I will often use my pressure canner, as it heats up faster and uses less water. In a water-bath canner: Process pint jars for 15 minutes and quart jars for 20 minutes. In a pressure canner: Process at 5 pounds of pressure, pint jars need 8 minutes and quart jars need 10 minutes.

STRAWBERRY JAM

Makes approximately 4 pints

Ingredients:

8 cups strawberries

3 cups sugar

zest from 2 lemons

¼ cup lemon juice

Directions:

Wash your jars and bands in hot soapy water, and leave them in the hot water until you are ready to fill them. Place the canning lids in a saucepan, cover them with water, and heat on medium-low. Fill the water-bath canner with water and put it on medium heat.

Mash the berries with a potato masher, blender, or immersion blender to the desired consistency. I prefer mine chunky, but my husband likes it more pureed.

Place all ingredients into a large pot. Stir until well combined. Bring the berries to a boil. Grandma's note: If the jam starts to foam, add a pat or two of butter to cut the foam.

Stir frequently to keep the sugar from scorching. Simmer the berries on a low boil for 10 minutes.

You can check the set of the jam by the sheeting test. Place a metal spoon in the freezer when you begin making your jam. After the 10 minutes of boiling, use the chilled metal spoon to ladle out a spoonful of jam. Hold the spoon and watch the way the jam drips off the spoon. If it's in little individual drops, the jam is not set. If it's in big goops, it's almost there. If it comes off the spoon in a sheet or doesn't really drop off at all, then the jam is set—yank that baby off the heat! Jam will continue to thicken up, or *set* in canning lingo, as it cools. Jam sets when it reaches 220°F. Though the sheeting test works, you'll get a more accurate reading with a thermometer. Use a large pot so your jam heats more evenly. If you have trouble reaching 220°F, you may need to add another ¼ to ½ cup of sugar. Be sure to closely monitor your jam so it doesn't scorch! Remove the jam from the heat as soon as it reaches the setting temperature.

Place your hot, clean jars on a dish towel. Fill the jars, leaving a ¼-inch headspace. A canning funnel will be your best friend during this part. With a clean, damp towel, wipe down the rim of each jar. Place the lids on and screw the bands down until finger tight.

Immerse the jars in a water-bath canner with the canning rack in place, making sure the water covers the tops of the jars by 1 to 2 inches. Once the water is boiling, set a timer for 10 minutes and allow the jars to process.

When the time is up, turn off the heat. After 5 minutes, remove the jars from the canner. Place them on a towel folded in thirds, in a draft-free area. Allow the jam to cool and set overnight or for at least 12 hours. Check the seals. If the center of the lid gives, then store it in the fridge and eat it soon. If jars are sealed, wipe them down with a damp cloth and store them in the pantry out of the light for up to a year.

OLD-FASHIONED BLACKBERRY JELLY

Makes approximately 6 cups

Blackberry jelly is probably my absolute favorite on fresh, hot-from-the-oven biscuits.

Ingredients:

> 1 gallon (16 cups) ripe blackberries
>
> 1 large green or slightly underripe apple
>
> 4 to 5 cups sugar

Directions:

Prepare your jars and lids (see page 101).

Chop up the apple and place it with the blackberries in a large pot. With a potato masher, mash up the blackberries. Boil the mixture for approximately 15 minutes. Blackberries will release their juices. Put this mixture through a sieve or food mill. You'll end up with about 6 cups of blackberry juice.

If you don't have a sieve or food mill, you can use a jelly bag or cheesecloth to strain the berries. Allow the boiled mixture to cool enough to handle and place it into the jelly bag or a few layers of cheesecloth. Tie the cheesecloth closed and hang it over a bowl to collect all of the juice.

Put the blackberry juice back into your pot. Stir in the sugar until it is completely dissolved. I always use less sugar to begin with and taste it before adding more. Bring it to a boil, then simmer for 10 minutes.

Fill prepared jelly jars with blackberry jelly, leaving a ¼-inch headspace. Wipe the rims clean and place lids and bands on your jars. Process them in a water bath for 10 minutes.

RED RASPBERRY AND CURRANT JELLY

Makes four 8-ounce jars

Ingredients:

1 cup red currant juice

3 cups red raspberry juice

¼ cup lemon juice

zest of 1 lemon

2 cups sugar

Directions:

In a saucepan, stir together all the ingredients. Bring the mixture to a hard boil and boil for 10 minutes, stirring often to keep the mixture from scorching. After 10 minutes, use the sheeting test to check the set of the jelly.

Depending on how ripe your berries are, I always recommend doing a taste test, especially with tart berries. Be careful, it's hot—don't burn your tongue. Add more sugar if desired.

If the jelly is still too runny, allow it to continuing boiling for 4 more minutes, and check it again. The longest I've ever had to let mine boil was 25 minutes. This jelly has always set quite firmly for me.

Once jelly has reached its jelled point, pour it into prepared jars, leaving a ¼-inch headspace. Wipe the rims clean and secure the lids and bands. Set the jars into a prepared water-bath canner. Bring the water to a boil and allow the jars to process for 10 minutes. Turn off the heat and wait 5 minutes before placing the jars on a towel folded in thirds. After 12 to 24 hours, check if they are sealed. If any jars haven't sealed, place them in the fridge to eat now, or store them in the freezer. Wipe the outsides of the jars clean and store them in a cool, dark place until you are ready to eat them.

If you don't wish to can your jelly, you can also freeze it for freezer jam.

A friend of mine had an overabundance of red currants and invited me to come pick them. They're a fairly tart berry, so we much preferred them in a jelly rather than straight off the bush.

We have a row of red raspberries on our homestead. Interestingly enough, our chickens don't seem to care for the raspberries. They like to lounge beneath their leaves for shade, but I've yet to catch one of them snitching a low-hanging ripe berry. But I've still got my eye on them, you can bet.

I paired the raspberries and red currants in a brightly festive jelly. The deep reds from both berries make me want to hang the jars from the branches of the Christmas tree. You did know I love Mason jars, right?

Pickling Basics

We've been talking sweets, but now we're moving into pickles. Pickling foods as a preservation method stretches back hundreds of years. Typically, most people think of cucumbers when they hear the word pickles, but pretty much every vegetable can be pickled.

Our favorite pickled foods are pickled asparagus and garlic. Our family has been known to pick a fight over who gets the last jar if we didn't put up enough. In fact, my siblings ask me for jars of our pickled asparagus as their Christmas gift.

It's important to note that the only way vegetables can be safely canned via the water-bath method is with pickling. This is because the vinegar brings the acidity level up enough to prohibit the growth of botulism. Always use 5% vinegar when canning and never lower the amount of vinegar used in a pickling recipe or change the vinegar ratio to water.

MELISSA'S PICKLING SPICE

Makes 2 Tablespoons

1 T. celery seed

½ T. whole black peppercorns

½ T. allspice

PICKLED GARLIC

Makes approximately nine 6-ounce jars

It's important to use pickling salt (also called canning salt) in this recipe as it doesn't have any additives that can discolor your food.

Ingredients:

135 cloves garlic (depending on the size of the garlic, about 15 per jar)

3 cups vinegar (5% acidity)

1½ cups water

2 T. pickling salt

9 tsp. mustard seed

9 tsp. black peppercorns

red chili flakes (optional)

Directions:

Peel your garlic. Fill your water-bath canner with water and begin heating on medium-high heat on the stove. You want to bring it to just below a boil. Wash your jars and bands in hot soapy water; leave the jars in the hot wash water until they're ready to be filled with garlic and brine. Pour the vinegar, water, and salt into a saucepan and bring it to a boil. Stir until the salt is completely dissolved.

Set the jars on a folded towel on the counter. Place 1 teaspoon each of mustard seeds and black peppercorns in each jar. Add a pinch of hot pepper flakes if you like a little heat in your food. (Whenever we make pickles we do two batches—one with added hot pepper for my husband and one without for me.)

Pack jars with the peeled garlic, leaving a ¾-inch headspace. Don't pack tightly. You want the brine to be able to flow around the heads of garlic. Pour hot brine over the garlic, leaving a ½-inch headspace. If you run short on brine, add vinegar to reach the proper level. Run a knife or spatula around the inner edge of the jar to remove any air bubbles.

Wipe the rims of the jars with a clean towel. Place canning lids on the jars and screw the bands down until they are fingertip tight. Set the jars into the canning rack and place them in the hot water bath, making sure at least one to two inches of water covers the top of the jars. Bring the water to a full rolling boil.

Start the processing time when the water reaches a full boil. Process the jars for 10 minutes. Turn off the heat and remove the lid for 5 minutes. Using a jar lifter, place the jars on a towel folded in thirds on a stable surface away from any drafts. Leave the jars for at least 12 hours. Check to see if they properly sealed. If any jars didn't seal, store them in the fridge.

Though we sometimes open jars of pickled garlic a week or two after making them, it's best to let them set for a month or so to develop their full flavor. Pickled garlic is wonderful to eat all by itself, but it is also good added to meat dishes, salads, or spaghetti. The brine is delicious poured over rice, in salad dressings, or in marinades.

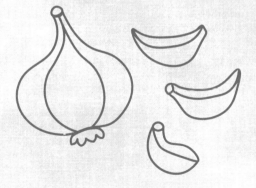

GARLIC DILL PICKLES

Makes approximately 4 quarts (or 8 pints)

Ingredients:

Pickles

7 to 8 pounds pickling cucumbers

ice

½ cup pickling salt

4 cups cold water

8 cloves garlic, peeled

8 tsp. whole mustard seed

8 to 12 heads fresh dill (or ½ cup dill seed or chopped dill weed

Brine

5 cups water

5 cups vinegar (5% acidity)

¼ cup sugar (more to taste if you prefer sweeter)

5 T. pickling salt

2 T. of your preferred pickling spices

Directions:

Wash the cucumbers well in cold water, gently scrubbing off any dirt. Remove ¹⁄₁₆ to ¼ inch from the blossom end of the cucumbers (enzymes around the blossom end will produce a softer pickle). You may also cut them into spears. Place all your cucumbers in a large glass or stainless-steel bowl. If you have more than a few layers deep of cucumbers, layer ice between the layers of cucumbers, if it's a smaller amount, place ice on top of the cucumbers.

Mix ½ cup pickling salt with 4 cups of cold water. Pour the salt water over the top of the cucumbers and ice, adding more cold water if necessary to cover the tops of the cucumbers. Place a clean plate on top of the cucumbers to keep them under the surface of the ice salt water. Fill a pint-sized Mason jar with water (use a lid) and set it on top of the plate to act as a weight. Put the bowl in the fridge to soak overnight or for 12 hours.

After soaking the cucumbers, pour out the salt water and rinse the cucumbers thoroughly with cold water and allow them to drain.

While the cucumbers are draining, begin heating up the water in your water bath canner. Place the brine ingredients in a large stainless-steel pot and bring it to a low boil, stirring to dissolve the sugar and salt. Allow the brine to simmer for about 10 to 15 minutes or until the spices have seeped into and flavored the liquid.

I prefer to use wide mouth quart jars when making pickles. Wash the jars in hot soapy water and then rinse. In each of your four quart-size jars, place 2 cloves of garlic and 2 teaspoons of mustard seed. (Halve those amounts for pint jars.). Using the larger cucumbers first, pack your jars, tucking the smaller cucumbers up around the top to a generous 1-inch headspace. Add your dill heads, slipping them down around the cucumbers.

Remove your spices from the brine and pour the hot brine over the cucumbers to a ½ inch headspace. Remove air bubbles and recheck your headspace. Add more brine if needed. Wipe the rims clean and put the lids and bands on, screwing down to fingertip tight.

Place the jars into a water bath or steam canner. Process quart jars for 15 minutes and pints for 10 minutes. After the processing time is finished, turn off the burner and remove the lid. Allow the jars to rest for 5 minutes in the canner with the lid off, then carefully remove the jars from the canner and place them on the counter on a folded kitchen towel (never place hot jars on a bare countertop as they can crack due to thermal shock). Allow the jars to cool for 24 hours, check the seals, and then store.

Pickles develop their flavor profile over a few months, so try to let them sit and deepen in flavor for at least a few weeks before eating them. (If you can. They're so tempting!)

PICKLED ASPARAGUS

Makes 6 quarts

As with any pickling, fresh vegetables will give you the best pickles and have the most crunch. A simple tip to see if asparagus is fresh is to snap it in half. It should break cleanly without any strings and you should hear a "snap" noise. If the spear is stringy or limp, the asparagus is not fresh.

We can eat a jar in one day just as it is, but pickled asparagus is wonderful when wrapped in a piece of ham or turkey with a filling of cream cheese. Be warned, they're so good you'll need to make more than one batch of pickled asparagus to last you through the year.

Ingredients:

180 spears of asparagus (depending upon size, about 30 spears per quart jar)

8½ cups vinegar (5% acidity)

4½ cups water

6 T. pickling salt

1 to 2 cups sugar

1½ tsp. celery seed

12 tsp. mustard seed

12 tsp. dried dill weed (or use 2 heads fresh dill to each jar)

12 cloves peeled garlic

red pepper flakes (optional)

Directions:

Place the water, vinegar, salt, sugar, and celery seed in a large pot and bring it to a boil, stirring until the salt and sugar are dissolved. Fill a water-bath canner with water and heat water to almost a boil.

Wash the jars in hot, soapy water. Wide-mouth jars are easiest to use when packing asparagus. Rinse the jars and place 2 teaspoons each of mustard seeds and dried dill (or two heads of fresh dill) and 2 cloves of garlic at the bottom of each jar.

Rinse the asparagus in cold water. Measure and chop off the ends so that the heads of the asparagus come to a ½-inch headspace of the jar. Pack them tightly. I find it easier to place jars on their sides when packing asparagus.

Once the jars are packed, pour hot brine over the asparagus to a ½-inch headspace. Run a knife or spatula around inner edge of jar to remove any air bubbles. Wipe the rims clean, set lids on top, and screw bands down to fingertip tight. Place the jars in your canning rack or basket and then into the water bath.

Bring the water bath to a rolling boil. Process the jars for 10 minutes. Turn off the heat and remove the lid for 5 minutes. Carefully remove the hot jars and place them on a towel folded in thirds in a draft-free area. Let them sit for at least 12 hours without touching.

Check to make sure the jars have sealed. If any have not, store them in the fridge. Try not to eat the asparagus for at least two weeks to allow the flavor to set, and wait six weeks for the fullest flavor to develop.

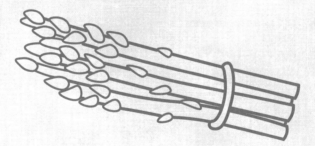

CHAPTER 4

BE PREPARED: PANTRY PROVISIONS

A well-stocked pantry in your dry storage, fridge, and freezer will not only be a blessing during hardships or emergencies, it will help reduce the temptation to spend more during each shopping trip on those items you tend to add to your cart whether you need them or not. When you are intentional about having extra supplies on hand, you can breeze right by those items and shelves and only buy from the planned list you have in hand.

I do my best to only go shopping once a month for the main part of our groceries. If I'm not in the stores, I'm not as tempted. When evaluating any purchase, ask yourself if it's an item you need (great!) or is it a good deal on something you didn't think you needed 30 minutes ago?

Beyond your dry-storage pantry, plan to have a regular store of supplies in a freezer, and aim for a faster turnover of items in your refrigerator. To help you plan, on the following pages I've included some detailed worksheets from my Homestead Preparedness course, which is part of my membership program, The Pioneering Today Academy. The *Tier* column is for you to decide where that item falls in importance to your family.

Tier 1: very important, must have
Tier 2: in a pinch we can do without, but we'd like to have it stocked
Tier 3: nice to have, but not a necessity
Tier 4: low priority or don't need at all

PANTRY GOODS

Baking Essentials

Item	Qty on Hand		Tier
Arrowroot Powder			
Baking Powder			
Baking Soda			
Butterscotch Chips			
Carob chips/nibs			
Chocolate Chips			
Chocolate, Baking			
Clear Gel			
Cocoa Powder			
Cornstarch			
Cream of Tartar			
Extract, Lemon			
Extract, Vanilla			
Extract, _____			
Extract, _____			
Gaur Gum			
Gelatin			
Potato Starch			
Salt, Kosher			
Salt, Sea			
Tapioca Starch			
White Chocolate Chips			
Xantham Gum			
Yeast			

Sugars

Item		Qty on Hand		Tier
Brown				
Coconut				
Corn Syrup				
Granulated				
Honey				
Maple Syrup				
Molasses				
Monk Fruit Sweetener				
Powdered				
Stevia				
Sucanat				
Yacon Syrup				

Beans/Peas

Item		Qty on Hand		Tier
Adzuki				
Baked Beans				
Black				
Black-Eyed Peas				
Cannellini				
Chickpeas (Garbanzo)				
Cranberry				
Fava				
Great Northern				
Kidney				
Lentils				
Lima				
Mung				
Navy				
Pinto				
Refried Beans				
Split Peas				

Snacks

Item		Qty on Hand		Tier
Breakfast Bar				
Crackers, _____				
Crackers, _____				
Crackers, _____				
Crackers, _____				
Granola Bar				
Nuts, Almond				
Nuts, Cashew				
Nuts, Peanut				
Nuts, Pecan				
Nuts, Pistachio				
Nuts, Walnut				
Nuts, _____				
Nuts, _____				
Nuts, _____				
Nuts, _____				
Protein Bar				
Seeds, Chia				
Seeds, Pumpkin				
Seeds, Sunflower				
Seeds, _____				
Seeds, _____				

Condiments

Item		Qty on Hand		Tier
Barbeque Sauce				
Cocktail Sauce				
Coconut Aminos				
Coffee Creamer				
Fish Sauce				
Hot Sauce				
Ketchup				
Lemon Juice, bottled				
Mayonnaise				
Mustard				
Salad Dressing, _____				
Salad Dressing, _____				
Salad Dressing, _____				
Salad Dressing, _____				
Salad Dressing, _____				
Salad Dressing, _____				
Salsa				
Soy Sauce				
Steak Sauce				
Tabasco Sauce				
Taco Sauce				
Teriyaki Sauce				
Vinegar, Apple Cider				
Vinegar, Balsamic				
Vinegar, Red Raspberry				

Item		Qty on Hand		Tier
Vinegar, Red Wine				
Vinegar, Rice				
Vinegar, White				

Soups

Item		Qty on Hand		Tier
Beef and Barley				
Beef Stew				
Broth, Beef				
Broth, Chicken				
Broth, Vegetable				
Butternut Squash				
Chicken				
Chicken and Rice				
Chicken Enchilada				
Chili				
French Onion				
Lentil				
Minestrone				
Mushroom				
Split Pea				
Tomato				
Vegetable				

Sauces

Item		Qty on Hand		Tier
Alfredo				
Cheese				
Curry Simmer Sauce				
Enchilada				
Marinara				
Red Curry Paste				
Spaghetti				
Tomato				

Dairy

Item		Qty on Hand		Tier
Condensed Milk				
Evaporated Milk				
Powdered Cheese				
Powdered Milk				

Beverages

Item		Qty on Hand		Tier
Almond Milk				
Coconut Milk				
Coffee				
Electrolyte Drink				
Hot Cocoa Mix				
Juice, _____				
Juice, _____				
Juice, _____				
Juice, _____				
Liquor, _____				
Liquor, _____				
Liquor, _____				
Liquor, _____				
Oat Milk				
Protein Drink				
Soy Milk				
Tea, _____				
Tea, _____				
Tea, _____				
Tea, _____				
Tea, _____				
Tea, _____				
Tea, _____				
Tea, _____				
Water				

Oils/Fats

Item		Qty on Hand		Tier
Almond Butter				
Avocado Oil				
Bacon Grease (Fridge)				
Butter, Powdered				
Coconut Oil				
Cooking Spray				
Flax Seed				
Ghee				
Hazelnut Spread				
Lard				
Nut Butter				
Olive Oil				
Peanut Butter				
Peanut Oil				
Schmaltz				
Sesame Oil				
Sunflower Oil				
Tallow				

Pasta

Item	Qty on Hand	Need Gluten-free	Tier
Angel Hair			
Bucatini			
Calmarata			
Capellini			
Cascatelli			
Cavatappi			
Cous Cous			
Egg Noodles			
Farfalle (Bow Tie)			
Fettuccine			
Fusilli			
Lasagna			
Linguine			
Macaroni			
Penne			
Ramen			
Ravioli			
Rigatoni			
Rotini			
Shells			
Spaghetti			
Tortellini			

Grains/Flours

Item	Qty on Hand	Tier
Amaranth		
Barley		
Bulgur		
Cornmeal		
Flour, All-Purpose		
Flour, Almond		
Flour, Amaranth		
Flour, Arrowroot		
Flour, Black Bean		
Flour, Bread		
Flour, Brown Rice		
Flour, Buckwheat		
Flour, Cassava		
Flour, Chickpea		
Flour, Coconut		
Flour, Corn		
Flour, Einkorn		
Flour, Fava Bean		
Flour, GF Blend		
Flour, Graham		
Flour, Green Pea		
Flour, Kamut		
Flour, Millet		
Flour, Oat		
Flour, Pastry		

Item		Qty on Hand		Tier
Flour, Quinoa				
Flour, Sorghum				
Flour, Soy				
Flour, Spelt				
Flour, Tapioca				
Flour, Teff				
Flour, Tigernut				
Flour, Wheat				
Flour, White Bean				
Flour, White Rice				
Millet				
Oats, Quick				
Oats, Rolled				
Oats, Steel Cut				
Popcorn				
Quinoa				
Rice, Basmati				
Rice, Brown				
Rice, Jasmine				
Rice, Long Grain				
Rice, Wild				
Sorghum				
Wheat, Einkorn				
Wheat, Hard Red				
Wheat, Hard White				

Item		Qty on Hand		Tier
Wheat, Kamut				
Wheat, Rye				
Wheat, Soft Red				
Wheat, Soft White				
Wheat, Spelt				

Spices and Herbs

Item		Qty on Hand		Tier
Cayenne Pepper				
Celery Salt				
Ceylon Cinnamon				
Chili Powder				
Cloves (Whole/Ground)				
Cumin				
Curry				
Ginger				
Mustard (Whole/Ground)				
Nutmeg				
Red Pepper Flakes				
Pepper				
Paprika				
Onion Powder				
Garlic Powder				
Turmeric				
Basil				
Dill				
Oregano				
Parsley				
Rosemary				
Sage				
Thyme				

Other

Item		Qty on Hand		Tier

Other

Item		Qty on Hand		Tier

EIGHT FOODS TO STORE AT HOME

While having a well-stocked pantry is smart, there are some items we should always have at the ready when the need arises. Having a stocked deep freezer doesn't do one any good if the power goes out for an extended period of time and all of that food is lost.

Our goal is to have close to a year's supply of our main staples on hand. These are the eight foods I believe you should be storing. I don't include fruits and vegetables, as most of us can grow or harvest these at home or close to our homes.

1. **Salt** can be used to preserve food as well as flavor dishes. I put salt at the top of the list because most of us don't have a way to get salt where we live, except at the store. We can all grow our own herbs, but most people do not have a naturally occurring salt source in the vicinity of their home. Store salt in a dry area, as moisture will make it cake together. If this happens, you can spread it out on a rimmed baking sheet lined with parchment paper. Depending on the time of year and your climate, you can use a warm sunny windowsill, or for those of us who live where sunlight can be scarce, preheat your oven to 250°F. Place the salt in the oven and then turn off the oven. Leave it in for 10 minutes, stir, and place it back in if needed.

2. **Fat.** Fruits and vegetables are part of a well-balanced diet, but our bodies require a certain amount of fat in order to function. We need fat for cooking and baking. I use butter, lard, coconut oil, and olive oil. Keep your fat source out of the heat and light. I put extra butter and lard in the freezer.

3. **Wheat berries.** You'll see flour on lots of food storage lists, but quite frankly, flour is not meant for long-term storage. It will go rancid and can also be a home for pests. Wheat berries and other forms of grain will store for years. Not only can they be ground into flour, but they can also be soaked and cooked into a cereal. We use about 100 pounds of wheat berries a year. I use hard white wheat and spelt as our primary type of wheat berries. Store wheat berries in a cool and dry location.

4. **Honey** is a nonperishable food. Raw honey is excellent for eating, cooking, and medicinal purposes. You can make a ginger-infused honey for medicinal purposes during cold and flu season. Honey is also excellent for baking. If honey hardens or forms crystals, simply place the container in hot water. Plus, honey just plain tastes good. I love to swirl it in my coffee. Store honey out of direct sunlight.

5. **Sugar** is needed in baking and also in canning homemade jams and jellies. However, I don't use regular processed white sugar. I use organic evaporated cane sugar, and all my jam and jelly recipes in this book use about a quarter of the sugar most recipes call for. Store sugar in a dry place in a pest-proof container.

6. **Dried beans** are not only inexpensive and easy to store, but they have huge nutritional value. Beans can be used in multiple dishes and should be stored in a dark, cool, and dry place.

7. **Oatmeal** is inexpensive and can be used for cereal, in baked goods, or even ground up into flour. It contains fiber and is easy to flavor with seasonal fruits and spices. We have oatmeal for breakfast at least once a week, if not more. Oatmeal is excellent with just cinnamon, a pat of butter, and a smidgen of sugar. We add peaches, blueberries, raisins, and other fruits as they come into season. Store oatmeal in a dry place.

8. **Coffee.** Most of us do not have a source of coffee available to us other than purchasing it. If you're a tea drinker, then stock up on your teas. But I am a coffee lover. While we could live without coffee, I'd rather have it on hand. Does anyone else just open the canister of coffee and take a big whiff? Whole coffee beans will store much longer than ground coffee and should be stored in a dry and dark area.

CHAPTER 5

COOK

Go, eat your food with gladness.

ECCLESIASTES 9:7

With today's mainstream society and the convenience of store-bought or processed ready-made food, cooking from scratch is becoming a lost art. Even many cookbooks contain processed foods in the ingredient list, like a can of condensed soup or packet of such-and-such mix.

Our great-grandparents cooked before there were mixes for everything, and the only canned foods they used were those they'd canned themselves. I realize not everyone can grow and can all their own food. However, you can still provide wholesome, from-scratch meals for your family. This chapter will show you how.

☙

I sat in the specialist's office.

We were determining why I had incredible esophageal pain that made my days and nights pure misery. I had been maxing out the medications for years without resolution and they were starting to cause their own damage.

The doctor handed me a stack of papers. "This is a list of foods to start cutting out."

I skimmed the first page. No coffee? No chocolate! No pick-me-up soda in the afternoon? I shoved the papers into my purse.

No doubt, the doctor had seen this response more than a few times. "Stick to the list and try to start tapering off your meds. I'll call you in a few weeks."

Later, when I was alone, I sat down and read through all the information, including my lab reports. The findings revealed that risky cellular changes were happening. I could squander this information and chance with stubbornness over foods I loved, or I could do what was hard but needed. I knew this was the time to get serious. God had given me this opportunity to change my health and I had the chance to bless my family with better, more-informed choices for them.

This pivotal moment led me on a path to examine all that I and my family were eating on a regular basis. I began to read the ingredient labels on everything. I figure that if I don't know how to pronounce an ingredient or don't know what it is, I'm not comfortable eating it or feeding it to my family. There are also plenty of known culprits, such as high-fructose corn syrup, in many options on grocery shelves.

Growing, harvesting, and cooking your own food reveals how miraculous and simple a nourishing meal can be. The food my family eats now is tastier and more satisfying, while actually serving these amazing bodies we've been given. It's been over twelve years and I can tell you I don't crave soda or processed foods. I feel better, sleep better, and I'm not bombarding my body with medications.

Whatever personal reasons you have for making changes, be encouraged that you can view food, choose food, cook food, and provide nourishment for your family in simple, doable steps. One planting season at a time, shopping trip at a time, one meal at a time, and one bite at a time.

As you go through this cooking section, my hope is that you will find some new favorite recipes and a few ways to give your old favorites a healthy update with a few substitutions.

REAL COFFEE, REAL CHOCOLATE, REAL FOOD

The beginning of my real-food journey began that day in the specialist's office. It started with cutting out soda, coffee, chocolate, and high fructose corn syrup. But it's continued to evolve and shape my life in ways I'd have never imagined.

First off, in case you were crying into your coffee for me, I found a way to still enjoy coffee almost daily. It's called a cold-brew system. You see, the oils in coffee contain most of the acid. Hot water brings these oils out into the coffee. But not so with cold-brewed coffee.

You take coarsely ground coffee grinds and pour cold water over them. Allow the mixture to steep for eight to twelve hours or overnight. Then strain it and store in the fridge for up to two weeks. You can also purchase a cold brewing coffee system with a filter, a container to brew the coffee, and a carafe for the strained coffee.

After the coffee is brewed with cold water, you can either enjoy it cold or add hot water or milk to make it a warm beverage. All I can say is I'm very happy to have found a way to enjoy my coffee without all the acid. And the frugal homesteading part of me adores the no-power-needed aspect.

I've also found I can eat dark chocolate. I do purchase an organic brand now and have found that eating a few pieces of dark chocolate (at least 70 percent cocoa) satisfies my cravings and doesn't bother my stomach.

These were the first items I cut out or switched, but it's been a journey in our home to find more natural and healthier products. In fact, the last time I went grocery shopping it dawned on me that I purchase hardly anything from the inner aisles of the store. I buy fresh vegetables and fruit, milk, cheese, nuts, and pantry staples such as salt, sugar, honey, and whole grains or seeds like quinoa. A far cry from the days of canned soups and boxes of nearly ready-made meals or desserts.

I have wisdom to share that I believe is very important: Don't let your food and eating become a religion. I've seen more heated debates about the kinds of food people eat than I have over politics. Some people only eat organic, some are gluten-free, some are dairy-free, some believe we shouldn't eat animals, and the list goes on and on.

I have fallen prey to this myself; don't think I'm exempt. When we're passionate about something, it's very easy to slip into thinking we're right. I've looked at things in lunch boxes and thought, *I'd never let my kids eat that.* I'm not always a pretty person on the inside. Left to myself, I'm judgmental and prideful.

But thankfully, God hasn't left me to myself.

While I do believe in eating healthy and caring for our bodies, it's not my job to reform everyone's kitchen. I can share changes we've made that have had a positive outcome, but I shouldn't condemn someone who doesn't eat or cook the way I do.

FLOUR

I began researching the flour we purchase from the store. Ever wondered why every package says "enriched with vitamins"?

Bear with me a minute here. Flour is made from a ground-up wheat berry. It's actually a hard kernel, not a squishy berry like a piece of fruit. This wheat berry is composed of three parts. The first part of the wheat berry is the bran, which is the hard outside part. The second part is the germ and holds the wheat oil. The third part is the endosperm, and this is the part regular flour from the store is made from.

Once the germ is exposed to air during the grinding process, it has a short shelf life before the oil turns rancid. Therefore, this part isn't used in store-bought flour, even whole wheat. However, it's where most of the vitamins and nutrients are stored. This is why store-bought flour says enriched with vitamins—because the natural ones have been taken out.

I grind most of our own flour at home now. I do purchase a small amount of organic all-purpose flour, because some baked goods just don't have the light texture without it. There are two types of grain mills for home use: a manual, or an electric grain mill. Both have good features, but what you intend to use them for will determine which is right for you. A manual grain mill doesn't require electricity and can be used with oil products like beans or nuts. An electric mill can grind a large amount of flour at once and can be adjusted with the flip of a switch. Whichever you choose, you'll be delivering your family a fresher, more nutrient-packed flour.

Have you ever noticed all the references to food in the Bible? Jesus is the bread of life. "Then Jesus declared, 'I am the bread of life. Whoever comes to me will never go hungry, and whoever believes in me will never be thirsty'" (John 6:35). Salt and yeast are mentioned in many verses. When you cook from scratch and understand how ingredients work, it helps us understand these verses even more. I love it when one aspect of life feeds into another . . . literally!

SALT

Salt is a funny thing. We need a small amount to heighten the flavor of whatever it is paired with. A bit of salt actually brings out the sweetness of desserts. Anyone else love salted caramel? Our food would be quite bland without salt.

One year I decided not to use salt when I canned our green beans. I really have no idea why I came upon this decision. It might have been some crazy notion to keep costs down, but I've since learned some things are worth the price.

The first jar I opened was so bland we couldn't eat it without adding salt. Normally, our home-canned green beans are the one vegetable my kids ask for and I have no trouble getting them to finish. My son said, "Mom, what's wrong with these?"

Since I'd canned them during the summer and we didn't start in on the current year's harvest until fall, I'd half forgotten about not adding the salt. "Nothing's wrong with them. Just eat your vegetables."

After filling all the water glasses and finally sitting down to eat my dinner, I forked up a large bite. My nose screwed up. "What's wrong with these beans?"

Then I remembered. No salt. I grabbed the saltshaker and passed it around. Even with the addition of salt, they still didn't taste the same as the jars with salt added at the time of processing. I learned an important lesson: Don't try to leave out the salt altogether.

YEAST

When I first began baking my own breads, I patiently waited for the dough to double in size. I nestled the dough in the mixing bowl, covered it with a tea towel, and set the timer so I'd be sure and remember to punch it down.

An hour went by and I lifted the corner of the towel. Um, wasn't the dough supposed to be almost to the rim of the bowl? Was my timer broken? (I have a natural inclination to assume it's never me but something else.)

Perhaps the dough wasn't warm enough. My woodstove ticked with heat. I plopped the stainless steel bowl on top of the stove, right next to the chimney. That ought to heat it up.

Another hour went by and I checked the dough. Still no rise. I dumped the dough out onto the counter to form it into two loaves. The bottom of the dough had a slight crust on it. Apparently I'd cooked the dough.

Fine, we'd eat unleavened bread because this stubborn—er, frugal—baker wasn't about to let all those ingredients go to waste. Still, a bit of time went by before I tried baking my own bread at home again.

Great bakers aren't born, they're taught. While some people do seem to have a natural knack in the kitchen, everyone learns by trial and error.

Thankfully, there are a lot of folks willing to lend their experience to the rest of us. So here's the thing with yeast: If the water's too hot you'll kill it, if the water's too cold it won't activate. Lukewarm water is best for activating your yeast. If your home is cool, you'll want to avoid using a metal bowl. Metal bowls cool quickly and don't retain heat as well as wooden or glass bowls.

The top of the refrigerator is often a warm place to let the dough rise, or you can turn on the oven light (not the oven) to create a warm incubator for your dough. And trust me on this: During the rising time, keep your dough off the top of the woodstove when it's burning!

Most recipes require two and a quarter teaspoons of yeast for the entire recipe. Worked through the batch of dough, it does its job, making the rest of the ingredients rise, which creates air pockets and the chewy lightness we desire in our breads.

LARD

Lard can be used just as you would use butter or coconut oil. I use lard in place of any recipe calling for shortening. Lard rendered at home is a good choice as it's not hydrogenated and doesn't contain dairy, so it is great for those with dairy sensitivities who need to avoid butter. Shortening, on the other hand, is highly processed and contains GMO products.

When rendering lard, I highly recommend only using fat from organic and pasture-raised pigs. Since we raise our own, I know exactly what's going into my lard. But my favorite reason for using lard is the flavor. It makes delightful pie crusts and pastry items.

I believe using things grown on our land or close to where we live is better not only for ourselves but for those in our community, and ultimately better for the country and the world. Growing coconuts where I live or olives to make my own oil is not a possibility. While I do use coconut and olive oil, it has to be shipped a long way to get to me. Many resources must be used to make the packaging, house the equipment to press the oil, and much fuel is used to ship it. I don't personally know the people or even the land it's being farmed from.

When we don't have pigs, I can get lard from our local butcher or another pig farmer. I believe supporting those close to home is important. I also receive joy in using a part of the animal that would otherwise be thrown out and wasted.

Baking with lard is pretty much the same as using coconut oil or butter, except it does tend to melt a tad faster. I add a bit more flour when using it in biscuits and pie crusts.

There are two types of lard. The lard around the kidneys and organs of the animal is referred to as leaf lard. This is considered the purest form and is the best for baking. The other lard is the back fat of the animal and is good for general cooking.

To get started, freeze the lard. It's easiest to work with if you freeze it first. Allow it to partially thaw for about two hours on the kitchen counter.

Chop it up in 1- to 2-inch cubes. You need the pieces of fat to be uniform to avoid scorching and uneven cooking. You want it small to release the oils. Some people will ask the butcher to grind the fat up first for easier rendering. Note: While chopping the lard, your knife and cutting board will become slick. Use caution!

Put ¼ cup of water in the bottom of your slow cooker. As the fat is starting to melt, you don't want it to scorch on the bottom. The water will cook off during the rendering. Fill your slow cooker with lard to the very top and cook it on high for 45 minutes to 1 hour. Once it starts to melt, turn down the slow cooker to low. My slow cooker tends to cook on the hot side, so I turn mine to low and leave the lid off for most of the rendering process.

Stir the lard every 20 minutes or so. After the liquid has reached the top of the lard, you're ready for the first rendering. Depending upon the amount of lard you're rendering, the time it takes for this to happen will vary. I did four and a half quarts at once and it took almost three hours for the first rendering. Place a strainer or sieve lined with a layer of cheesecloth over a large bowl. Pour the rendered lard through. Put the contents of the strainer/sieve back in the slow cooker and continue cooking.

Allow the rendered lard to cool for approximately ten minutes. After the lard has cooled, pour it into wide-mouth Mason jars. If you don't wait for the lard to cool a bit, you run the risk of cracking your jars. Let the lard continue to cool to room temperature before putting on lids and placing in the fridge. Be sure to wipe down the outside of the jars to remove any grease residue.

Mark the first rendering. I simply use a permanent maker and put a 1 on the lid for the first rendering and so on for the next two. Your first rendering is the most pure. It will have virtually no pork flavoring and is perfect for baking pastries, cookies, and cakes. The second rendering will be slightly darker in color and is still fine for biscuits, pie crusts, corn bread, and more savory dishes. The third rendering will be the darkest, has the most pork flavor, and is best used as a cooking oil for frying. All the renderings will be yellow in their liquid form, but will turn white as they cool. Once solid, the first rendering will be snow white.

Store your lard in the fridge. Lard should be fine on the shelf, but I prefer to store mine in the fridge to avoid having any of that work turn rancid. It's good in the fridge for six months. The jars I'm not using go in the freezer where they'll stay good for at least a year.

OTHER PANTRY ESSENTIALS

It is freeing to practice self-sufficiency and preparedness. Even if you only choose a few of the staples mentioned in the special pantry section, you'll notice the ease that comes with having your most basic foods available to you when cooking. The pantry checklist covered the dry goods. Below is a list of the other foods that are handy to have in your refrigerator and freezer. If you are lucky enough to have a spare fridge and freezer, you can plan even further ahead.

Leavening product

Active dry yeast (store yeast in the fridge for best results)

Acids

I purchase whole lemons and limes when they're on sale and freeze them whole for use throughout the year. They're also wonderful when fermented to use in savory dishes.

concentrated lemon juice	lime juice whole lemons	whole limes

Dairy

milk	buttermilk	kefir
cheese	yogurt	

Nuts

Unsalted raw nuts are best as you can roast them, make your own candied nuts, make your own nut butters, toast them for texture in soups or on casseroles, add them as toppings for muffins, cakes, and breads, or eat them plain.

Meat

Using bone-in cuts or whole poultry will allow you to then make your own stock and broth after you've used the meat. What we don't raise ourselves, I purchase either organically or grass-fed. At the very least, I look for no-hormone or no-antibiotic labels.

beef	poultry	lamb
pork	fish	

MAKE IT FROM SCRATCH

Truthfully, I've found it much more frugal to make dishes myself from scratch. The food tastes better, and when you count the time it takes to drive to the store, park the car, take kids to the bathroom, go through the aisles, wait in line at the checkout, get kids and groceries into the car, start to pull out from the parking lot, only to have kids say they have to go potty again, it's faster to make it at home as well.

After numerous power outages in our area of the country—and after a mudslide took out the main highway for almost three weeks—I've also learned the benefit of having a food supply at home. Not only does it help when the store isn't open or we can't get to it, but it also saves me time by allowing me to shop from our pantry instead of the store shelves.

HOMEMADE WHITE SAUCE, GRAVY, OR CONDENSED CREAM OF SOUP REPLACEMENT

Makes about 1 cup, to replace 1 can of store-bought condensed soup

I can make a few cups of sauce to replace those cans of condensed soups in three minutes for about fifty cents, and that's using organic ingredients. Here's my recipe for replacing condensed cream soups in your dishes. It also makes a really good white sauce for pizza.

Ingredients:

3 T. butter (coconut oil if you're dairy-free)

3 to 4 T. flour (organic cornstarch or arrowroot powder for gluten-free)

1 cup milk (for a richer sauce, use cream; for a dairy-free option, use chicken broth)

¼ tsp. salt

dash of pepper

Directions:

In a saucepan, melt butter (or your fat of choice) over medium-low heat. Whisk in the flour. It will make a thick paste. Slowly whisk in your liquid. Bring it to a simmer (barely a boil), adding more liquid if it becomes too thick. It will thicken up a bit as it cools. Remove the pan from heat and stir in salt and pepper.

You can add in sautéed mushrooms for a cream of mushroom flavor. Sauté minced garlic and onion for another flavor add-in, depending upon your dish.

If the sauce is too thick, add more liquid; too thin, add in a little bit more flour (or other thickener) and allow it to simmer for another minute or so. Be sure to stir frequently to avoid scorching the bottom of the sauce. The longer it cooks, the thicker it will become.

DINNER ROLLS

Makes 16 rolls

Ingredients:

½ cup warm water

2¼ tsp. yeast

½ cup buttermilk

1 egg

½ cup butter, softened

¼ cup honey

1 tsp. salt

2 cups whole wheat flour
(2½ cups if using spelt)

1¾ cup all-purpose flour

Directions:

Pour warm water over yeast in a large bowl. Let it sit for 5 minutes or until foamy. Add the buttermilk, egg, butter, and honey. Stir in the salt and flours. Knead for 6 to 8 minutes. If you are not using a stand mixer with the kneading attachment, place a little bit of olive oil on your kneading surface. Adding too much flour when using whole wheat results in a dense product.

After kneading, place the dough in an oiled bowl, cover it, and let it rise for an hour.

Punch down the dough and form it into rolls. Place the rolls in a large cast-iron skillet. When rolls are touching, it forces them to rise up instead of out. Place the rolls in your oven with the light on and allow them to rise about 45 minutes, or until doubled.

Remove the skillet from the oven and preheat the oven to 400°F. Bake for 12 to 15 minutes. As soon as the rolls come out of the oven, brush them with a stick of butter.

Don't have buttermilk? Because let's face it, sometimes the whim to bake hits when we're least prepared. But because we've got our pantry stocked, we can make a substitute for buttermilk by mixing in a tablespoon of lemon juice or apple cider vinegar to a cup of milk. Stir and let it sit for a few minutes. When the milk curdles and turns thick, you're ready to add it to your dough or batter.

HONEY WHOLE WHEAT
BUTTERMILK SANDWICH BREAD

Makes 2 loaves

Store-bought bread is another item I replaced with homemade. After going through all the ingredient labels at the store, I was appalled at the long list of things in our bread, high fructose corn syrup and loads of sugar being just some of many.

I'm going to let you in on a little secret. Buttermilk. Yes, buttermilk is a cultured food that makes many folks turn up their nose. I mean, have you tasted it? It's sour. (My father loves the taste of straight buttermilk, so for those of you who do, he's right there with you.) But it does delightful things to baked goods. Buttermilk makes your baked goods lighter, and the texture—oh, the texture. You'll have to try it to believe it, but buttermilk is my go-to.

This is my favorite honey whole wheat buttermilk bread recipe. It makes scrumptious sandwiches and worth-getting-out-of-bed-early French toast.

Ingredients:

4½ tsp. yeast

1½ cups warm water

¼ cup honey

2 cups buttermilk

6 T. melted butter

1 egg (optional)

8 cups freshly ground hard white wheat (or 9½ cups all-purpose flour)

1 T. sea salt

scant ¼ cup vital wheat gluten (Omit if using all-purpose or bread flour. Vital wheat gluten gives whole wheat flour a better rise, but it's optional.)

Directions:

Mix yeast, warm water, and honey in a mixing bowl. Let the yeast proof for about 5 minutes. (Proofing means the water turns frothy and the yeast is active.) Add in the rest of the ingredients until the dough starts to pull away from the side of the bowl. Knead with dough hook for 4 minutes if you are using a stand mixer. If kneading by hand, knead for 6 minutes.

Let the dough rest for 10 to 15 minutes. Lightly coat the counter or kneading surface with oil to keep the dough from sticking.

Turn out the dough onto your prepared surface and knead it by hand for another 5 minutes. Grease a large glass bowl, put the dough inside, and cover it with a tea towel. Place the bowl in a warm area and allow the dough to double in size, about 1 hour.

Punch down and divide the dough into two equal parts. Place them in greased loaf pans, cover with a tea towel, and let the dough rise until it has doubled again.

Bake at 375°F for 25 minutes. Pull out the loaves and immediately take a stick of butter and rub it over the top of the bread. Allow it to cool on racks. Try not to eat both loaves in one sitting.

If your kitchen is cool or you're not getting the rise you want, preheat your oven to 400°F. Bake the bread for 5 minutes before lowering the temperature to 375° and then bake as directed. This trick works with any bread recipe as the extra heat kicks the yeast into overtime action.

HOMEMADE CORNBREAD

Serves 8

There are two kinds of cornbread. Southern and not-southern. Southern cornbread is made without sugar and with white cornmeal. My grandmother was a true Southern lady and firmly stated yellow corn was for livestock and white corn was for humans. I use whatever cornmeal I have in the cupboard, but she was adamant about this.

If you want to make it Southern-style, omit the sugar.

Whichever way you make it, I promise you'll never want to go back to those little boxes of mix.

Ingredients:

½ cup butter

1½ cups all-purpose flour (may substitute 2 cups freshly ground spelt flour)

2 T. sugar

1½ T. baking powder

½ tsp. baking soda

½ tsp. salt

¼ cup coconut oil or lard

1 cup cornmeal

2 eggs

1 cup milk

Directions:

Preheat the oven to 350°F. Place ½ cup butter in an 8 x 8-inch baking pan or an 8-inch cast-iron skillet. Put it in the oven while it's preheating, to melt the butter. Remove it when the butter is melted—this will grease the pan for you. If you happen to forget and the butter turns brown and starts to boil, no worries. Just use a hot pad and pull out the pan when you remember or when you hear it popping in the oven . . . whichever comes first. One could use a timer, but life's more exciting in the kitchen without it.

In a large mixing bowl, combine the flour, sugar, baking powder, baking soda, and salt. Cut in the coconut oil or lard. Add the cornmeal. Stir in the eggs, milk, and melted butter from the skillet. Mix until just combined, but don't over-stir the batter.

Pour the batter into your greased pan. Bake for 30 minutes or until the center is set.

TRAYER WILDERNESS FAVORITE GLUTEN-FREE BREAD

Makes 2 loaves

I've done a small amount of gluten-free baking, but I am in no way an expert at it. So I asked my good friend Tammy from TrayerWilderness.com to share her favorite gluten-free bread recipe with us. Tammy's family is strictly gluten-free, so I knew she'd have a well-tested recipe for us.

Ingredients:

4½ cups warm water

⅓ cup Sucanat or organic sugar

2 T. (2 packages) active dry yeast

1 T. salt

2 T. olive oil or melted butter

6 cups Better Batter Original Blend flour (BetterBatter.org)

Directions:

Mix the water, sugar, yeast, salt, and olive oil and let it sit for 10 minutes to sponge.

Add the flour two cups at a time and beat vigorously after each addition. Gluten-free flours need to be worked over hard. The dough will not be like regular wheat flour dough that you can handle. Use a spatula to transfer it to two loaf pans. Wet your hands with warm water and press the dough into the pans, smoothing the surface of the bread.

Let it rise for an hour. Heat the oven to 350°F and bake until the surface is brown—roughly 30 to 40 minutes.

HOMEMADE TORTILLAS

Makes 8 tortillas

I don't know anyone who doesn't like tacos. My son is a picky eater, but if I wrap it in a tortilla, he's good to go.

However, a pack of eight tortillas can cost close to seven dollars at the store. Have you ever read the ingredient list on them? It's not so good.

Good news, tortillas are easy to make at home and cost a fraction of the price. I can make a batch of tortillas at home for less than a dollar.

The first time I made tortillas, my husband was a bit skeptical. However, after the first bite, he said, "These are so good you could sell them."

Ingredients:

> 2 cups whole wheat flour
>
> 1 tsp. sea salt
>
> ¼ tsp. baking powder

> 2 T. coconut oil or lard
>
> ¾ cup warm water

Directions:

Measure out the dry ingredients in a mixing bowl. Cut in the fat with a pastry cutter until it's absorbed into the flour. Pour in the water and mix until it just holds together. If the dough is too sticky, add another pinch of flour. If it's too dry, add water, one tablespoon at a time.

On a lightly floured surface, knead the dough for 2 minutes. Cover and let it rest for 20 minutes or longer. Resting the dough is important for the texture and ease in rolling it out. You can skip it if you're in a hurry . . . totally been there, but truly, letting it rest will deliver a better tortilla. Mix the dough in the morning to save time on busy nights.

Ready to roll?

Preheat a cast-iron skillet on medium heat. I usually preheat two so I can cook more than one tortilla at a time.

Divide the dough out into eight balls. Lightly spread olive oil on your counter. Place the dough ball on the counter and push it down flat with the heel of your hand. With a rolling pin, roll out into a thin circle.

Place one tortilla in a heated cast-iron skillet. When small bubbles start to appear, flip the tortilla over. It will take approximately 2 minutes on each side. Have a tea towel or paper towel-lined large plastic bag ready to put hot tortillas into. This will help keep them pliable, and nothing is better than a fresh warm tortilla. I've been known to eat the first few before they even make it to the bag or towel.

If you have any left, store your cooked tortillas in the fridge for another meal. You can also double the recipe if you have a large family or someone like me who likes to snitch a few extra tortillas before the meal is served.

I've used hard red wheat, hard white wheat, spelt, and mixtures in these tortillas. You can also use regular all-purpose flour, but we prefer the whole wheat in this recipe.

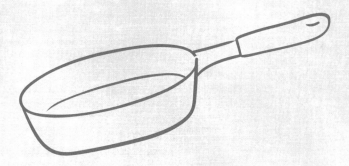

HOMEMADE YOGURT

Makes 4 to 6 cups

Making yogurt at home is easy, more frugal than buying it at the store, and yogurt can be used in almost any recipe in place of milk or mayonnaise. Did you know that yogurt made at home also contains more live cultures than store-bought, because it's fresher?

You can use yogurt with a live culture in it from the store or order a starter online. There are many kinds of starters, even ones for dairy-free people! I purchased mine from CulturesForHealth.com.

Because I love all things heirloom, I went with an heirloom Bulgarian yogurt starter. It's a sweeter flavor than Greek yogurt, making it more versatile in our home.

Ingredients:

4 to 6 cups whole milk (do not use ultra-pasteurized, preferably non-homogenized as well)

¼ cup yogurt (with live cultures) or a yogurt starter

Directions:

Pour the milk into a saucepan. On medium-low heat, bring the milk to 160° to 175°F. (A higher temperature will result in a thicker yogurt.) Hold this heat for 15 minutes.

Allow the milk to cool to 110°F. A layer of scalded milk will form on the top; skim this off with a spoon.

When the milk reaches 110°F, pour it into a clean glass Mason jar (or jars). Add the starter and thoroughly mix it in. Put a lid on your jar. Keep the yogurt between 100°F and 110°F for 4 to 6 hours. There are a few ways to do this. You can purchase a yogurt maker, but I prefer the more frugal route when possible. I've filled my slow cooker with three inches of water and turned it on the "keep warm" setting with the lid off. This setting keeps the water at 110°F, and you can place the jars in the water. Another option is to wrap up your jars in a thick bath towel and put them in the oven. The oven works as a natural incubator. Both options work well. Just don't forget your yogurt is in the oven and turn it on!

After three to four hours, check to see if the yogurt is thick. Once it's reached the desired thickness, store it in the fridge for up to one week (if you don't gobble it up within a day or two).

If your yogurt separates too much with a lot of whey (watery liquid) on top, then your yogurt got a little too hot while fermenting. Try keeping it slightly cooler. You can either stir the whey back into the yogurt or drain it to use as liquid in cooking or fermenting.

Homemade yogurt isn't generally as thick as store-bought yogurt. My kids like really thick yogurt, while I prefer mine creamier. If you want your yogurt to be thicker without straining off any of the whey, right before you put your yogurt into the fridge (while it's still warm) stir in a tablespoon of gelatin. Use 1 tablespoon of gelatin per quart of yogurt. A whisk works well to avoid clumps of gelatin in the finished product.

Use yogurt in your smoothies, with fruit, in oatmeal, and in place of sour cream or mayonnaise in any recipe.

Make sure to save a ¼ cup of your fresh yogurt as your starter for your next batch. I freeze ¼ cup of starter so I don't have to remember to save it later and so that the starter is at its strongest point, right after it's been fed.

I recommend only using whole milk for everything. Whole milk has fewer sugars in it than skim or two-percent milk, which means less of a spike in your blood sugar. Also, many of the vitamins in milk are contained in the fat. Plus, it just tastes better!

HOMEMADE BONE BROTH OR STOCK

Yield varies

Making your own stock or bone broth is an easy and frugal way to get more out of food you've already purchased. Purchasing a whole chicken or roast with the bone in is cheaper than purchasing the same amount of meat in boneless skinless or prime cuts.

We usually cook one whole chicken a week or other large bone-in cut of pork or beef. I can make several meals from that and then I take the leftover bones and make my own stock. These bones would have been thrown out, but by making my own stock or broth I'm stretching them even further. Bone broth also contains collagen and gelatin, which are nourishing for our bodies.

Ingredients:

1 or 2 chicken carcasses or a few pounds of beef bones

¼ cup apple cider vinegar

onion, garlic, or other vegetable odds and ends

herbs of choice (I like rosemary, sage, thyme, oregano, and basil)

water

Directions:

Place the bones in a large pot or slow cooker. Pour ¼ cup apple cider vinegar over the bones and let them sit for a half hour or so. Cover the carcass with water and bring it to a boil. Then switch to a low simmer, and add vegetables and herbs.

I cook mine in the slow cooker for 12 to 24 hours or on top of our woodstove in a large stockpot. You can let it simmer for up to 48 hours—whichever suits you and your schedule.

When finished, pour the broth through a fine-mesh sieve or cheesecloth. You can reuse the bones and make a second batch of stock if you wish. Discard the cooked vegetables. Allow the broth to cool and pour it into clean Mason jars. Store it in the fridge for up to a week, freeze it, or can it.

I use our homemade broth as a base for soups, gravies, and sauces, and to cook quinoa or rice. It adds a depth of flavor and also vitamins and minerals.

HAM AND BEAN SOUP

Serves 10 to 12

This is one of our favorite soups to make with a leftover ham bone. The best part is, this frugal soup costs less than a dollar a serving but doesn't skimp on taste. I've had both my husband and my readers tell me this was the best soup they'd ever had.

Ingredients:

1 ham bone with meat	1 cup sliced celery
1 cup diced onion	4 cups white beans
3 cloves garlic, chopped	4 cups water
1 cup diced carrot	dash of salt and pepper
1 cup chopped rutabaga or parsnip	

Directions:

Chop up all your vegetables in fairly even pieces so they cook at the same rate.

Put your ham bone in a large stock pot or Dutch oven. Dump in all your vegetables. Add the beans (undrained if using canned, drained if you soaked dried beans the night before). Pour in 4 cups of water.

Bring the liquid to a low simmer on the stovetop. Allow it to simmer for about 2 hours, stirring every now and then.

Once meat is falling off the bone, transfer the bone to a plate. Using tongs, pick off any good chunks of meat remaining on the bone and put the meat back into the soup. Add a dash of pepper and salt. Serve.

If you want to make this soup in the slow cooker, cook it on low for 3 to 4 hours. If you cook it too long in the slow cooker, it tends to lose the flavor from the vegetables and turn too mushy.

HOMEMADE REFRIED BEANS

Serves 8

Beans are a great way to stretch the budget. They're also extremely frugal. We love to eat these as they are, in tortillas, with chips, and just about any way you can shovel them in.

I can up our shelled October beans in the fall just to make this on nights I'm pushed for time. (Many people know them as cranberry beans.)

You can also use dried beans and soak them before cooking. Place the beans in a large bowl and cover them with warm water. Many people like to add a tablespoon of lemon juice or apple cider vinegar to the soaking water to help aid in digestion. Let the beans soak for up to 24 hours. Drain and rinse thoroughly.

Ingredients:

- 1 T. olive oil or other fat
- ½ medium onion, chopped
- 3 cloves garlic, minced
- 2½ tsp. chili powder (or more, according to taste)
- 1 tsp. garlic powder
- 1 tsp. cumin
- salt and pepper, to taste
- 1 quart canned October beans (or 4 cups of any bean of your choice)
- 1 cup water or chicken broth

Directions:

In a large saucepan over medium heat, place a tablespoon of olive oil, bacon grease, lard, or coconut oil and coat the pan. The lard gives the beans a true, authentic taste.

Sauté the onion for three minutes. Add the garlic and spices and continue sautéing for one to two minutes. Add the beans to the pot. I don't drain my home-canned beans. I only use a minimal amount of salt in canning and the juice in the can adds flavor on its own to recipes. If you are using store-bought or dried beans, soak them the night before, drain, and rinse. Add water or chicken broth. Bring the beans to a simmer and cook for five minutes.

Mash the beans with either an immersion blender or a potato masher. If the beans have too much liquid, allow them to simmer with the lid off for a few minutes.

HILLBILLY BEANS

Serves 10 to 12

My son requested this recipe after coming home from the neighbors and seeing their dinner. He promptly named them Hillbilly beans.

Ingredients:

2 cups pinto or red beans

2 cups white beans

1 pound ground beef

1 medium onion, minced

4 cloves garlic, minced

1 (16 ounce) jar tomato sauce

¼ cup molasses

3 T. brown sugar

¼ cup apple cider vinegar

2 tsp. salt

2 tsp. dry mustard

Optional: garlic powder and onion powder, to taste

Directions:

Soak your beans the night before, and drain them after soaking. Place the beans, ground beef, onion, and garlic in the slow cooker. In a glass measuring cup, mix together the tomato sauce, molasses, brown sugar, vinegar, salt, and mustard. Pour the mixture into the slow cooker. The liquid should just cover the beans and beef. Add more water if needed. Cook on low for 8 hours.

Taste before serving. If you like a stronger savory flavor, add a teaspoon of garlic and onion powder just before serving. You can also add a few pieces of bacon. I tend to think bacon makes everything taste better, but with the cost of bacon on the rise, it makes the dish more expensive.

These beans are wonderful served with corn bread, in a tortilla, or over nachos.

SAUSAGE AND POTATO SOUP

Serves 8

Ingredients:

1 pound sausage

½ medium onion, diced

3 cloves garlic, minced

3 T. flour

3 cups broth or milk

2 cubed potatoes

1 to 2 carrots, diced

2 cups green beans

2 cups corn (optional)

salt and pepper, to taste

3 fresh sage leaves, coarsely chopped (optional)

Directions:

In a large stockpot or Dutch oven, brown the sausage, onion, and garlic over medium heat. Add in the flour and stir until the flour has absorbed the grease. Pour in your choice of liquid. I've oftentimes done half broth and half milk, or even all broth. Whisk until the liquid is incorporated with the flour mixture. Add in the vegetables and seasonings, and bring to a low simmer. Simmer for a half hour or until the vegetables are cooked all the way through.

Feel free to substitute any vegetable for another depending on what you have on hand, what's in season, or your family's preferences.

The sausage gives the soup an out-of-this-world flavor. You might be tempted to lick your bowl clean.

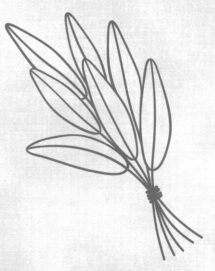

GRANDMA'S CHOCOLATE MAYO CAKE

Serves 12

Anyone else have a sweet tooth? I love to bake. Desserts are what make my kitchen go round. I used to purchase boxed cake mixes by the half dozen when they came on sale. Until (you guessed it) I started reading the ingredients.

I went back through our family recipes and came across my great-grandmother's chocolate cake recipe. This comes together super quick and tastes better than its processed boxed counterpart. After all, if a recipe has survived this many years, you know it has something going on.

The secret is the mayonnaise and the coffee. The coffee heightens the chocolate flavor, and in my opinion, something can never taste too chocolatey. You don't taste the coffee in the finished cake.

Ingredients:

2 cups flour (I use soft white wheat but all-purpose or cake flour is fine)

1 cup sugar

½ cup cocoa

1 tsp. baking soda

1 tsp. baking powder

¾ cup mayonnaise

1 egg (optional—use when making cupcakes)

½ cup cold water

½ cup brewed coffee

1 tsp. vanilla extract

Directions:

Preheat the oven to 350°F.

Grease and flour two 9-inch cake pans or cupcake tins. Stir all the dry ingredients together. Combine the wet ingredients with the dry and stir until smooth. Pour the batter into the prepared pans, and bake for 30 to 40 minutes for a cake or 16 minutes for cupcakes. Cool completely before frosting.

CARAMEL FROSTING

Makes 1½ to 2 cups

Homemade frosting is one of those things you'll never go back to the can for. The flavors, the options, the dive face-first into the bowl . . .

Frosting is pretty basic. You have the fat source, the sweetener, a liquid, and extracts or chocolate. Oh, but the flavors we can make.

This frosting gives a slight caramel flavor that pairs oh-so-nicely with chocolate. Is there anything that doesn't pair nicely with chocolate?

Ingredients:

5 T. butter

1½ cups brown sugar

3 T. boiling water

1 tsp. vanilla extract

Directions:

Beat the butter and slowly add in the sugar until they are creamed together. Pour in boiling water and beat until creamy. Add vanilla and beat again. Spread the frosting over a cooled cake or cupcakes.

CREAM CHEESE FROSTING

For 18 cupcakes or 1 full-size cake

I can't stand a frosting recipe that doesn't make enough to frost an entire cake. Or perhaps I use too much frosting . . . no, there's no such thing. This makes enough frosting to generously frost enough for a crowd.

Ingredients:

8 ounces cream cheese, softened

3½ cups powdered sugar

½ cup butter, softened

2 tsp. vanilla extract

Directions:

Cream together all the ingredients until smooth. If you don't have powdered sugar, simply run regular sugar through a blender or spice grinder for a finer texture.

UPSIDE-DOWN UPRIGHT APPLE CAKE

Serves 12 to 16

If you're my husband, the only cake needed in the world is chocolate. However, I'm not that partial and happen to love all cakes. I especially love ones that create a lovely syrup in the bottom so I don't have to deal with frosting. Every girl needs a go-to cake when she's in a hurry. If you add fruit, it makes it healthy, right?

I first made this cake for church. I intended it to be an upside-down apple cake, but I pulled it out of the oven right before we left for church and didn't have time to invert it. And the Upside-Down Upright Apple Cake was born.

Ingredients:

½ cup coconut oil

¾ cup brown sugar

4 cups sliced apples, tossed in sugar
and cinnamon

2 cups all-purpose flour (or 2½ cup
spelt flour or 1¾ cups whole wheat
pastry flour)

1 cup sugar

2 tsp. baking powder

½ tsp. cinnamon

¼ tsp. nutmeg

¼ tsp. ginger

¼ tsp. salt

2 eggs

1 cup buttermilk

2 tsp. vanilla extract

Directions:

Place the coconut oil in a 9 x 13-inch pan and set it in the oven. Preheat the oven to 350°F. Pull out the pan when the coconut oil is melted. Sprinkle brown sugar over the coconut oil. Spread the apples out evenly in the pan. (You can use fresh or frozen apples. If frozen, thaw the apples in the fridge before using them in cake.)

Mix together the dry ingredients. Add in the liquids and stir until just combined. Pour the batter evenly over the apples. Bake for 25 to 30 minutes or until a toothpick inserted into the cake comes out clean.

Allow the cake to cool, then invert it or serve it upright.

GRANDMA'S FLAKY PASTRY AND PIE CRUST

Makes four 9-inch pie crusts

This is my great-grandmother's pastry and pie crust recipe. It is the best pie crust I've ever had. In fact, when I was little, I wouldn't eat pie crust. Until we went to my great-grandmother's and I tasted hers. After my mother switched out her recipe to this one, I ate all of my pie crust.

I've even been known to roll out this pie crust, sprinkle it with cinnamon and sugar, and bake it without a filling. Yep, it's that good.

Ingredients:

4 cups all-purpose flour (or 5 cups spelt flour)

1 T. sugar

2 tsp. salt

1¾ cups cold butter, lard, or coconut oil

1 egg

½ cup very cold or ice water

1 T. apple cider vinegar

Directions:

Combine the dry ingredients. Cut in the butter, lard, or coconut oil. You can even use a mixture of the different fats. Add your egg and liquids, stirring until the dough just holds together. Do not overwork the dough.

Chill for at least 15 minutes.

Divide the dough into four equal parts. Turn out one piece at a time onto a lightly floured surface or wax paper. Roll to ⅛-inch thickness. Bake with your favorite pie filling.

If you are making a cream pie or need a pre-baked pie shell, you'll want to do a blind bake. This means chilling your dough, then rolling it out and placing the bottom crust in your pie plate.

Preheat the oven to 375°F.

Line the prepared pie crust with a piece of parchment paper and then fill it with dried beans. Lightly press the beans against the sides of the crust to keep the dough from shrinking while it bakes.

Bake for 14 to 16 minutes, until the edges of the crust begin to brown. Remove the crust from the oven, lift out the bean-filled parchment paper, and allow the crust to cool.

You can also freeze the dough. It thaws well in the fridge and will be nicely chilled for rolling out.

Note: Whichever fat you use, it's important that it be very cold. You get flaky pastry when the fat melts as it's baking, not when you're mixing. I've even used frozen butter and grated it on the largest hole of my grater.

GRANDMA'S APPLE PASTIES

Serves 10

Nowadays we can have a fresh apple whenever we want. Almost all fruit is sold year-round in the aisles of our grocery stores. But when folks used to only eat what they'd put up themselves, they didn't always have apples to make a pie.

During the Great Depression my father's mother cooked with what they had on hand. The old gnarled trees of her orchard still stand sentinel in the fields of the old place at our family's homestead. Even when the apples in the barrels had been used up, the shelves still held applesauce. This recipe is how my grandmother would make apple pasties for a treat when the apples were all gone.

Ingredients:

2 flaky pastry crusts   **lard or coconut oil for frying**

1 pint applesauce

Directions:

Melt lard or coconut oil in a large cast-iron skillet over medium heat. Roll out two chilled pie crusts on a lightly floured surface. Using a biscuit cutter, cut out small circles of dough and spoon a few tablespoons of applesauce into the center of one round. Place a second circle of dough on top and use the tines of a fork to crimp the edges closed. Fry the pasties in the hot oil until cooked, working in small batches, flipping over to cook each side.

Place cooked pasties on a towel and allow them to cool before you devour them. You can also sprinkle a dash of cinnamon and powdered sugar over the pasties when they come out of the oil.

OLD-FASHIONED APPLE PIE

Serves 8

If the word *homemade* had a taste, it would be of apple pie. Never underestimate the delight it will bring when you place a hot apple pie and some ice cream on the dinner table.

Ingredients:

2 pie crusts (recipe on page 168)

3 cups sliced apple (about 3 to 4 medium apples)

1 T. flour

⅓ cup sugar

½ tsp. cinnamon

¼ tsp. nutmeg

butter

Directions:

Preheat the oven to 400°F.

Roll out one pie crust and line a 9-inch pie plate or cast-iron skillet. Mix the apples with the flour, sugar, cinnamon, and nutmeg, then turn the mixture out into the pastry-lined pie plate. Top the filling with four to six pats of butter.

Roll out the top pie crust and place it over the filling. Crimp the edges of the pastry closed, and cut slits to allow the steam to vent. Brush the top of the crust with a bit of milk or cream and sprinkle it with a light dusting of sugar.

Bake for 50 minutes.

FROM-SCRATCH CHICKEN POT PIE

Serves 6

Ingredients:

2 flaky pastry pie crusts

2 cups cooked, diced chicken or turkey (dark meat adds more flavor)

2 cups mixed vegetables (cooked or frozen)

½ cup diced onion

3 T. butter

2 T. flour

1 cup milk (substitute chicken broth or, for a truly decadent treat, use cream)

¼ tsp. salt

dash of pepper

Directions:

Preheat the oven to 375°F.

Roll out one pie crust and line the bottom of the pie plate. Melt the butter in a saucepan over medium heat and cook the diced onion until translucent, about 3 minutes. Stir in the flour and form a paste. Slowly whisk in the milk. Bring it to a low simmer; the sauce will thicken as it cooks. If it becomes too thick, add more milk. If it's too thin, add another tablespoon of flour. You want a fairly thick sauce.

Add the cooked poultry and vegetables to the pastry-lined pie plate. Pour the sauce over the vegetables and poultry. Place the top pastry crust, crimp the edges, and cut slits in the top pie crust to allow venting. Place it in a preheated oven and cook for 45 minutes or until the pie crust is golden.

CHICKEN AND BROCCOLI BISCUIT BAKE

Serves 10 to 12. You can make this recipe as it is written for a gluten-free option, or use my flaky buttermilk biscuit recipe (page 174) for the biscuit topping.

Ingredients:

Casserole

2 cups cooked, diced chicken

1 head broccoli, cooked and in pieces

salt and pepper, to taste

2 T. butter

3 cups chicken broth

½ tsp. onion powder

½ tsp. garlic powder

½ tsp. xanthan gum

1 cup mayonnaise

1 tsp. curry powder

1 cup shredded cheese

Biscuit Topping

½ cup coconut flour

½ cup almond flour or tapioca starch

2 tsp. baking powder

1 tsp. garlic powder

½ tsp. onion powder

½ tsp. salt

½ cup shredded Colby Jack cheese (you can use any type of cheese you like)

¼ cup melted butter

4 eggs

¾ cup sour cream or unsweetened yogurt

Directions:

Preheat the oven to 350°F.

In a 9 x 13-inch pan, layer the chicken and broccoli. Sprinkle with pepper and salt (I just shake a light amount on top from the shaker without measuring).

In a large saucepan or skillet, melt the butter and pour in the chicken broth. Bring it to a simmer, then whisk in the onion and garlic powders and the xanthan gum. Let it simmer for a minute and add an additional ½ teaspoon xanthan gum if needed to thicken the sauce (it will thicken slightly upon cooling).

Once the sauce is thickened, stir in the mayonnaise and curry powder. Pour this over the top of the chicken and broccoli.

Sprinkle an even layer of grated cheese over the top.

To make the biscuit topping, first combine the dry ingredients in a large bowl. Use a fork to mix in the Colby Jack cheese a few tablespoons at a time.

Add the rest of the ingredients (your wet ingredients) and fold together until it forms a dough. You'll want to fold it over and stir pretty well to get all of the ingredients incorporated.

Take a large spoon and drop dough by the spoonful on top of the casserole to cover the top; if needed, you can take the back of the spoon to smooth it out to make an even layer.

Bake the casserole in your preheated oven for 30 to 35 minutes, until the biscuit tops are golden.

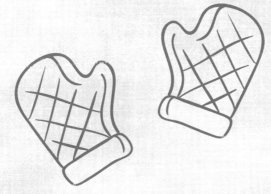

FIVE COMMANDMENTS FOR FLAKY BISCUITS

1. **Thou shalt use buttermilk.** The higher acid content does wonderful things to the texture of baked goods, especially in no-knead baked goods like pie crust and biscuits. Buttermilk is your secret to flakiness. Both this recipe and a recipe to make your own cultured buttermilk are just two of the over 100 recipes found in my book, *Hand Made*. If you don't have buttermilk, you can take 1 cup of milk and add 2 tablespoons of lemon juice, and let it sit until it is nice and thick.

2. **Thou shalt only use cold butter.** I've tried frozen butter and didn't like the texture as well as when I've used cold butter. Nor did I like the little flakes from grating it. Take it straight from the fridge and cut it into cubes right when you are ready to mix it in. This is a must.

3. **Thou shalt not overhandle the dough.** Overhandling the dough creates tough hockey puck biscuits. Follow the instructions exactly for best results. (I sound like I could be a drill sarge huh?)

4. **Thou shalt only use a metal biscuit cutter.** I know you've been told you can use a cup turned upside down, but that results in short squatty biscuits. No one wants a squatty biscuit. It pinches the edges of the biscuit down so it can't rise. You, my friend, deserve mile high biscuits.

5. **Thou shalt not be a biscuit twister.** When you push the biscuit cutter down, don't twist—this, too, pinches the sides. Push straight down and lift straight up. Boom! Ya got this.

Note: You can cut out the biscuits, place them on a cookie sheet and freeze them for 15 minutes, then place them in a freezer container. To bake them from frozen, put the biscuits in the cast-iron skillet or baking sheet and increase the baking time by 3 to 4 minutes.

FLAKY BUTTERMILK BISCUITS

Makes 8 biscuits

This recipe is from my book *Hand Made* but originally it is from my mother. Her biscuits were always good, and then one day she called me and said, "You've got to try my new biscuit recipe. I've tweaked it and can't believe how light and flaky they are now."

As you'll see once you try these, she wasn't joking. I've tossed out any other recipe I had and have used this one for years now.

Ingredients:

2 cups all-purpose flour	½ cup (one stick) butter
1½ tsp. baking powder	2 tsp. honey
½ tsp. baking soda	1 cup buttermilk
½ tsp. salt	

Directions:

Preheat the oven to 400°F.

Mix up your dry ingredients and then bring your butter out from the fridge. Cut it lengthwise in half, then in half again, and then cube it up.

Use a pastry cutter and work in the butter until it looks like itty-bitty pea-size clumps coated in the dry ingredients.

Add the honey and ¾ cup of the buttermilk till it sticks together on itself. If you need to add the rest of the ¼ cup, go ahead, but it should be a shaggy type of dough, not smooth.

Lightly dust the countertop with flour and dump out your dough. Gently pat it into a ½-inch-thick rectangle. It should be slightly tacky; if it sticks to your fingers, lightly (and I mean lightly) dust the top with flour.

Fold the dough into thirds, turn it vertical, and pat it back out into a rectangle. Repeat the process two more times, for a total of 3 times patting and folding. This helps create those delicious flaky layers.

After the final pat and fold, roll the dough to a 1-inch thickness and cut out your biscuits. You should get six biscuits, and then you can push the scraps back together and pat out the dough again to cut the last two biscuits. If you don't want to reroll the scraps after cutting out circular biscuits, you can roll out the biscuit dough into a rectangle and use a sharp knife to cut square biscuits.

Place the biscuits in a cast-iron skillet (or on a baking sheet) and bake for 15 minutes or until they are golden on top.

GARDEN-FRESH TOMATO SOUP

Serves 4

There is absolutely no reason to buy cans of condensed soup. Instead, stock some pantry basics and easily make your own with healthy ingredients. This homemade tomato soup is one of them. I use the items I've canned from my garden, but you can also make it with store-bought versions of these ingredients. You can easily double the recipe for a bigger batch.

Ingredients:

2 cups tomato sauce

2 cups bone broth

½ tsp. salt

1 T. nutritional yeast

1 tsp. garlic powder

1 tsp. onion powder

¼ cup heavy cream

parmesan cheese, to taste

oregano, to taste

Directions:

Pour the tomato sauce and bone broth into a pot, then stir in the salt, nutritional yeast, garlic powder, and onion powder. Place the pot on the woodstove or over medium heat on the stove and bring to a simmer. Remove from the heat, stir in the cream, and ladle into bowls. Garnish with shredded parmesan cheese and oregano.

HOMEMADE VANILLA EXTRACT

Makes 8 ounces

Ingredients:

7 to 10 vanilla beans

8 ounces vodka or rum (I like the flavor the rum gives the vanilla)

Directions:

Run a knife lengthwise down the center of the vanilla bean to open it up. Chop the vanilla bean into 1-inch pieces. Place the chopped vanilla beans into a clean pint-size Mason jar. Pour alcohol over the beans until they're completely submerged. Put a lid on the jar, and shake.

Place the jar in a cool, dark spot (I use our cupboard near the sink where we store our coffee). Shake it every few days or so for about six weeks. You can go longer for a more intense flavor. Once the extract has reached its desired strength, strain out the used beans and store the extract in a clean glass jar. I purchased a couple of swing-top glass bottles to store my extract in and put one whole split bean inside to infuse a little extra flavor. Bake up as many wonderful things as you can imagine!

HOMEMADE MINT EXTRACT

Makes about 8 ounces

Ingredients:

¾ to 1 cup of mint leaves

vodka

Directions:

Rinse the leaves and pat them dry. Roll and crush each leaf between your fingers to release the oils. Alternatively, you can roughly chop them. Place the crushed or chopped leaves in a clean glass jelly jar.

Pour vodka over the top until the leaves are fully submerged. Place the lid on your jar and give it a good shake or two. Store the jar in a dark cupboard and shake it every few days.

Allow the leaves to steep for at least six weeks, or longer for a stronger extract. Once the extract is at the desired strength, strain out the leaves and store the extract in a clean glass jar, out of sunlight and away from heat. For gift giving, I like to use a small chalkboard label to pretty up the jar.

You can make extracts with other flavors in a similar manner, using fresh or dried leaves. I grow several kinds of mint and each variety will create a slightly different-tasting extract. When using fresh leaves, it's best to pick the leaves in the early morning when they contain the highest concentration of the oil.

CHAPTER 6

CLEAN

Finally, brothers and sisters, whatever is true, whatever is noble, whatever is right, whatever is pure, whatever is lovely, whatever is admirable—if anything is excellent or praiseworthy—think about such things.

PHILIPPIANS 4:8

Many of today's cleaning products, for our homes and our bodies, contain dangerous chemicals. We shouldn't have to worry about what we're using to clean our items! I don't want my home or my life filled with harmful things, including my cleaning cupboard.

The pioneers didn't have aisles of cleaning and personal care products to choose from. They used simple ingredients to meet all their cleaning needs, and you can too. In this section, I share easy cleaning recipes for every aspect of your home.

In high school, I was hired to clean house for an elderly couple who lived up the road from us. I'm kind of surprised they hired me. I'd never kept house before and knew very little about cleaning. On my first day, the woman pointed me to the spray can of oven cleaner.

I followed the directions and scrubbed a long time to remove the built-up grease.

Happy to be done and have good results, I headed back home. But as the day wore on, the skin on my hands started to burn. Red blotches scattered across my hand and wrists. Days later, they were still raw and painful.

My mom examined my sores. "Didn't you wear gloves when you cleaned the oven?"

I shook my head. "I didn't know I was supposed to."

Lesson learned. It took a week for my skin to heal.

In our homes and lives, there are so many unhealthy, even dangerous things we use daily. We can wear gloves and hope we're protected, but we'd be better off if we never came into contact with these hazards.

After I had children, my concern about chemicals weighed on me.

When my children were infants and learned to crawl, I examined my entire home from a different level. I crouched down and viewed my home from the floor. Afterwards, no dangling items remained, heavy things within grasp were removed, and the cleanliness of my floors became a priority. After all, babies have this neat habit of putting not just their hands in their mouth, but also their feet. Did I want my children's sensitive skin to come in contact with remnants of these harsh chemicals?

Nope. Nada. Not one bit. Was I going to stop cleaning my home? No.

I began looking into natural cleaners. I knew my great-great-grandparents hadn't browsed the aisles at the general store for their favorite brand of cleaner. What had they used?

There are two natural ingredients most of us already have that can be used to clean just about every surface of our homes: vinegar and baking soda. These two have become a staple in my home and cleaning closet. And if they aren't in yours, they will be soon. Even swapping out one of your usual cleaning supplies with a homemade recipe will save you money and will show you how these simple ingredients can make your home shine.

FROM-SCRATCH CLEANING

I usually use white vinegar for cleaning, but I always have raw apple cider vinegar on hand for cooking and health reasons. Whichever you happen to have

HOMEMADE CITRUS ALL-PURPOSE CLEANER

Some people don't particularly like the scent of vinegar while cleaning. As it evaporates, the smell leaves, but if you want your cleaner to smell a little bit better, you'll want to try this next recipe.

Fill a quart-size canning jar three quarters full with **4 to 5 citrus peels** (I usually use lemon). Pour 3 cups white vinegar over the lemon peels. Let it set for a minute and then top it off with more vinegar to completely submerge the lemon peels. Cover the jar with a lid and band and set it in a dark cupboard for two weeks. Shake the jar every few days. You might want to mark the top of the lid with the date in case you forget when you started.

In two weeks, pour the vinegar through a strainer or cheesecloth. Dilute it in a spray bottle with two parts water to one part lemon vinegar. Use this on windows, countertops, mirrors, and as a general multipurpose cleaner. You can use any citrus fruit, or add some herbs for your own unique custom blend.

If you don't have any citrus peels, you can add ten drops of your favorite lemon or orange essential oil.

can be used. White vinegar is usually a bit cheaper, so I like to use it for cleaning. Here are some of my recipes for using vinegar and baking soda to clean.

Window Cleaner

Take a spray bottle, fill it a quarter of the way with **vinegar**, and then top off the bottle with **water**. I've used this cleaner with paper towels and washable rags, and it cleans my sliding glass door, the mirrors, and all the windows without a single streak. Now that my son is old enough to help with chores, I don't worry if he goes a little bit spray-happy or happens to get some on himself while cleaning.

> **NOTE:** To make a homemade pine cleaner, fill a quart-size canning jar with freshly clipped **pine tips or branches**, and pack it tightly. Pour **white vinegar** over the top and cap it with a lid. Allow the pine to infuse the vinegar for four weeks in a dark cupboard.
>
> After the infusing time, pour it through a strainer or cheesecloth, and dilute it in a spray bottle with two parts water to one part pine-infused vinegar. For an extra boost of pine scent and degreaser, add a few drops of pine or fir essential oil.

Floor Cleaner

Ever notice small dark spots in the divots of your linoleum? Over time, soap builds up and dirt sticks to it. Using vinegar eliminates these spots. If you have little ones or pets, you won't have to worry about their exposure to chemicals where they play.

Add about **a cup of vinegar** to your bucket or sink full of **water**. No soap. Use this solution to mop your hardwood, laminate, tile, or linoleum. (It is not recommended to use acid-based cleaners, such as vinegar or citrus, on limestone and marble.)

HOMEMADE LIQUID LAUNDRY DETERGENT

4 oz. bar of soap, grated (I choose a natural soap scented with lemon)

4 cups of boiling water

2½ gallons of hot water

1 cup Borax

1 cup washing soda (not to be confused with baking soda)

½ cup Oxiclean or other powdered bleach that is safe for colored clothes (this is optional, but it provides more stain-fighting power)

¼ cup baking soda

20 to 30 drops essential oil (optional)

Find yourself a big pot or bucket. I used a five-gallon bucket to mix up my soap. Grate your soap into your bucket. Add 4 cups boiling water. Stir until all the soap is dissolved. Hot tap water doesn't dissolve the soap or the powders enough. You may wish to wear gloves to prevent burns from the hot liquid.

Add the rest of the hot water, Borax, washing soda, powdered bleach, and baking soda. Stir until all is dissolved. It will be kind of goopy. Add the essential oils after everything else is dissolved, and mix well. Let it sit overnight, stirring occasionally as you remember. I leave it in the corner of the kitchen so I'll be sure to see it and stir.

I keep some of the soap in the bucket with a lid on, but I pour some into half-gallon wide-mouth Mason jars to keep above the washer for easier dispensing. I'll tell you what, everything just looks better in a Mason jar. It's my number-one decorating go-to.

Use ⅓ to ½ cup per load. It doesn't suds up like commercial soap, so don't be worried you did something wrong if you don't see suds. This kind of threw me the first few times I used it (as I was used to the suds), but it doesn't affect the cleaning ability.

The main cost of this detergent is the bar of soap as the other ingredients cover multiple batches. I chose a handmade lemon-scented bar from our local co-op, as I wanted the detergent to be as natural as possible but still smell good. I got my powdered bleach at the dollar store. The other items can be found online or on the laundry detergent aisle of most grocery stores.

Laundry Solutions

Add **¼ cup vinegar** to your laundry instead of bleach. It will kill odor-causing bacteria and clean your washing machine with no discoloring. I toss mine into the liquid softener dispenser. Wash clothes in cold water. If they're really grimy, you may want to use warm water. For most loads, cold water works fine. I promise you, we don't go around with dirty, stinky clothes.

Use a clothesline or drying rack. During the good-weather months, I use a clothesline. This cuts down my power bill by at least fifty dollars per billing cycle. If you  can't string a clothesline, then try using a drying rack. Plus, there's something about hanging up each article of clothing that soothes me. I oftentimes say a prayer for the wearer of each garment.

I also advise making your own laundry detergent. You're probably wondering if it really cleans the clothes and if it's cheaper than store-bought. Yes to both. Our clothes never smell funny (unless I've left them wet too long in the washer and had to rewash them, which is not frugal at all, but happens occasionally), the dirt and grime wash out the same as with store-bought detergent, and it only costs $4.50 for three gallons of soap.

Drain Unclogger

Vinegar is also an awesome way to unclog drains. Pour **⅛ to ¼ cup of baking soda** down your drain. Follow it with a chaser of **vinegar**. I pour until it reaches a good foam, allow it to foam for a few seconds, and chase it again with more vinegar. Let your drain sit for ten to fifteen minutes. Pour **a cup of boiling water** down the drain. For an especially clogged drain, repeat. I do this every other month or so to keep the pipes clear.

Carpet Cleaner

Dampen stains with the **all-purpose cleaner** (page 181; test a small area first for discoloring). Blot up the spot with a rag. If the carpets have an odor, sprinkle **baking soda** over the carpet, let it sit for 15 minutes, and then vacuum.

> **FRUIT FLY TROUBLES**
> If you're having fruit fly troubles, this can clear up the problem. Fruit flies often lay eggs in your sink pipe. This will kill any eggs and help eliminate those pesky buggers. This past fall, I couldn't get rid of the fruit flies for anything. I set traps, locked up my fruit, and still had a few buzzing around. Within 24 hours of the baking soda and vinegar treatment, we were fruit fly free!

Faucets

Wet a towel in **vinegar**. Wrap it around the faucet and handles and let it sit for a half hour . . . or until you walk back in the room and remember you were cleaning. Use the towel to wipe the faucet clean. Hard water stains and gunk will be gone.

Shower and Bathtub

I use **baking soda** to scrub the bottom of our shower and the tracks of our shower door. After rinsing off the baking soda, I spray all the surfaces with my **vinegar rinse**. I let it sit for a few minutes and then wipe it clean.

Sinks

Sprinkle **baking soda** into your sink. Mix it with a small amount of **water** to make a paste, and scour the sink. It eliminates odor and rubs off stains. Rinse clean with warm water.

Toilets

Dump ½ cup **baking soda** into the toilet bowl. Let it sit for about fifteen minutes. Scrub it with a toilet brush. This takes away any odor and scours off anything undesirable. Spray the toilet seat, handle, and base with the **home-made all-purpose citrus cleaner** and wipe clean.

Dirty Dishes

Ever have baked-on food stuck in your pans? Liberally sprinkle on **baking soda**. Use the baking soda to scour off baked-on food. It absorbs the grease as you scrub. I've found this works best with a dry pan and no added water.

I use mostly cast-iron cookware. Because soap can ruin a good seasoning, I use a salt scrub to remove cooked-on food. Sprinkle **a few tablespoons of salt** onto the cast iron and scrub. Dump the soiled salt into the garbage and then rinse the pan with hot water. Dry and lightly oil the cast iron before putting it away.

Natural Oven Cleaner

Knowing firsthand what commercial oven cleaners can do to the skin, I was determined to never use them again. But when we were having Thanksgiving at our home, I couldn't leave my oven in its current state of messiness. Nothing makes me give my house a good cleaning like having company over. (I'm not sure if this means I should invite people over more often or clean my house more. Either way, I can get a month of Saturday cleanings done in a few hours if company is on the way.)

This method works extremely well and requires a small amount of elbow grease. Liberally sprinkle **baking soda** on the inside of your open oven door. Scrub it with a dry rag or even your fingertip. It's safe and won't harm your skin. The dry baking soda absorbs the grease, and the grit of the powder lifts it off. I tried it with water, and it didn't work as well as the dry method for me. Especially soiled spots may need another dousing of baking soda.

Next, apply baking soda to the bottom of the oven. I did have to make a light paste with baking soda and water for the sides and top of the oven, but they usually don't have as much baked-on gunk. Use a hand broom to sweep off the soiled, dry baking soda.

Wipe any remaining residue with a damp cloth. You can also spray it down with your vinegar cleaner. Any spots that still have baking soda will foam, and you can wipe them up.

I did try the foaming action to lift up the grease, but all it did was foam. It is fun for the kids to watch, but not so effective in getting the gunk up.

☙

If you dedicate a little time each day to housekeeping, you'll stay on top of it. While I can't put in an hour every day, I can always find fifteen minutes. When I'm truly focused, it's amazing what I can get done in just that short amount of time. I hate to leave dirty dishes on the kitchen counter. But some nights I'm so tired that the thought of it makes me want to hurl them all into the garbage and use paper plates.

However, I can usually clean up those bowls and pots with five minutes of dedicated scrubbing. Oftentimes we build up a chore in our minds as taking much longer than it really does. Make a plan to put a little effort into house-keeping every day and see how much you can get done.

CHAPTER 7

RAISE

I am the good shepherd. The good shepherd lays down his life for the sheep.

JOHN 10:11

Raising any animal teaches you a lot about yourself. The Bible verses about shepherding take on a whole new level of meaning when you've actually experienced taking care of a flock! Raising animals has taught me many important faith lessons.

While raising livestock is work—and harder for some, depending upon your location—most folks, even those in an urban setting, can raise some type of livestock. I share tips and considerations on choosing livestock, frugal options and ways to cut down on feed bills, and how you can incorporate raising livestock into your life and home.

❧

I grew up on a cattle farm. During the winter evenings, after my father got home from hauling logs up the road to our barn, I went with him to feed those cattle. To this day I can close my eyes and remember the sweet, musty scent of hay and the spongy feel of loose hay squishing beneath my booted feet.

In the beginning of winter, the stacks of hay stretched clear up into the rafters of the old barn. I scaled those stacks as nimbly as Spiderman ever dreamed. Then with my leg strength, I'd push the bales so they toppled with a muffled thud to the ground where my dad would then load them into the truck.

I was only nine when my dad taught me to maneuver a stick shift. I also learned not to pop the clutch. If you've ever thrown your dad off the back of a truck, you'll quickly develop the finesse of slowly letting the clutch out while feathering the gas.

While I drove the truck, my father tossed the hay off the back like bread-crumbs. The head of the herd filed in first, jostling for position for the first bites. Younger cows kicked up their heels and bounced along the edge of the herd until more hay was tossed for them, never remembering from the night before that everyone got fed.

When we were done, I'd bring the truck to a stop and slide over. Dad would climb in, smelling of hay and freshly cut wood, the perfume of a farmer and logger rolled into one. Rough hands warmed against the heater vents. He'd roll down the driver's side window and drive back along the line of cattle, headlights shining like lanterns, reflecting in the cattle's eyes. His gaze traveled over them, counting and noting which cows looked close to calving. If some were missing, we went looking. It didn't matter that he'd been up since three that morning. We'd drive along the mountainside and down to the pond, searching for the lone cow.

Our cows weren't our pets, but if they were in trouble, they knew we were there to help.

Whether you raise four different kinds of animals or have one chicken coop, the labor and commitment involved will result in gratitude and respect for the sustenance of God's creation. And because we know the level of care it takes to watch over and provide for mere animals, we better understand a smidgen of what God does for us.

GETTING STARTED

Two things to ponder when considering raising livestock:

First, which animals to raise. There are many options, from laying hens, meat chickens, beef cattle, pigs, sheep, goats, rabbits, or even fish in ponds or large tanks. Laying hens are great because if you purchase hens instead of chicks, you're getting food every day from the get-go. The other livestock offer larger amounts of food, but keeping some of them will be dependent on where you live and the amount of acreage you own. Goats can provide milk and meat. Rabbits are a good meat source, and they breed quickly. If you've never had rabbit, it tastes just like chicken. Sheep can be used for both their wool and meat. Fish provide meat as well.

Second, consider the end game. This will help you decide which livestock animals to start with. Do you want dairy animals? Then a goat or cow will be your choice. Do you want enough meat to feed your family for an entire year with one animal? Then beef cattle or pigs will most likely be your choice.

Don't want to spend an entire year or two caring for an animal? Then consider meat chickens that are ready to butcher and eat in as little as eight weeks. We raise Cornish Cross chickens as our meat bird. Many folks also like Freedom Rangers, though they take longer to reach butchering weight.

All animals will require some type of shelter, water, feed, and a pen or fencing. Obviously, the larger the animal, the more space and feed will be required.

When it comes to pasture, remember that the recommended acres per animal varies greatly by climate (and therefore the growth rate of grass). Here in the Pacific Northwest, generally one to two acres is all that's needed for cattle, but in certain areas of Texas you'd need eight acres per cow. Research this per your geographical location. We prefer to not tax our pastures and do a two-acre minimum per head (even though we could push it at one acre).

I've also found that when chickens are given extra space, they are much less likely to peck and pick on one another. The more cramped their conditions, the more territorial they are inside the coop and pens.

Almost all animals (especially herd animals like cattle) need a friend. Same with pigs, sheep, and chickens. They find safety within a herd, and when left by themselves they will not only be lonely but may have anxious behavior as well.

When evaluating animals and space, consider the average annual amounts of meat needed per family of four. Factors include the age of your children, how often your family eats meat, how much of each type of meat you eat at a specific meal, and how many times a week or month you eat each meat type.

Animal	Square foot needed for shelter per animal	Square foot for run out/exercise pen per animal	Acreage needed per animal	Average need for a family of 4 per year
Broiler (meat chicken)	3 to 4 sq. ft.		N/A	25
Cattle- Beef/Dairy	75-100 sq. ft.	100-125 sq. ft.	1 to 2	¼ to ½ beef, 1 dairy cow
Dairy Goat	20-25 sq. ft.	50 sq. ft.	¼ to ⅓	1 to 2
Laying Hen	3 to 4 sq. ft.	10 sq. ft.	N/A	6 to 8
Pig	48 sq. ft. with exercise yard; (double if no yard provided)	200 sq. ft.	N/A	1 to 2
Rabbit	5 sq. ft. (7.5 sq. ft. if nursing)		N/A	48
Sheep	20-25 sq. ft.	50 sq. ft.	¼ to ⅓	6

Mob Grazing

If you practice pasture rotation, you can raise multiple animals on the same square footage. A good example of this is from Joel Salatin's practice of mob grazing with cattle followed by chickens.

Mob grazing is sectioning off the amount of acreage the cattle will eat down in a 24-hour period (or a few days). If allowed access to the entire acreage, a cow will cherry pick what it eats, like a toddler who chooses to eat ice cream all day unless forced to eat the vegetables on their plate. When cattle are allowed full range to acreage, they'll eat the choicest pieces of grass, leaving behind all other forage types. Grass needs a good sixty days to replenish its roots once it's been cut/eaten/grazed, but if they are allowed, cattle will come back and bite that same tender shoot again in a few weeks, continually weakening the grass in the pasture and allowing the weeds to become more prevalent.

Instead, when they're on a smaller section of pasture, they'll eat everything in that space over 24 hours. The next morning, they're moved onto fresh pasture and not allowed access to what they just ate for ideally another eight weeks.

A few days after you move the cattle from that section of pasture, put your chickens on it. They will scratch up the cow poop and eat the larvae (fly eggs) beginning to hatch in the poop. Their manure will also drop on that pasture. This, along with their scratching, will help distribute both the cattle and the chicken manure.

This system requires you to use a chicken tractor. It's a moveable run out pen (we built a small coop and nesting box on top of ours) that is fully enclosed so the chickens are protected from predators and only eat where you need them to, but because you can move it to fresh grass every day, they get the benefit of free ranging and eating all the bugs and fresh grass and seed heads they desire. This method also eliminates smell, because you're not piling up manure.

Since we began implementing Joel's mob grazing strategy, our pastures have never produced so well or been so healthy, and therefore, neither have our animals. It also allows us to raise cattle and chickens on the same acreage.

Clearing Pasture

Consider using pigs to clear pasture or brushy areas. Unlike goats, who eat back brush, pigs root it up from the ground. In the case of blackberries (which are a noxious weed where we live, they're so prevalent), goats did not kill them but simply pruned them back. However, the pigs rooted them up and killed them.

We use the pigs to naturally till up areas that need to be reseeded or have the brush removed. We don't have to do the work, their manure adds to the soil, and we get bacon out of the deal at the end! That's a win folks.

BUTCHERING

The chart at right will let you see at a glance how long it takes common livestock to reach the average size for butchering. Again, these are averages. While you can absolutely butcher any animal at home, beef is best when dry aged in specific temperatures, and without a controlled area to hang it, you won't get as good of flavor or texture (or worse, it could spoil).

Also, the larger the animal, the more equipment it takes. A full-size pig will need to be scalded, so a tractor is needed to hoist it above the scalding tank, submerge it, and lift it back up again. While many homesteaders do have tractors, I'm not considering it something most people have on hand, and therefore pigs don't fall into the category of "easily" butchered at home.

The chart will also help you determine which animals to start with based on your space available, how long you wish to wait to harvest, and hiring or not hiring out the butchering.

Animal	Easily Butcher at Home	Requires Acreage	Time to reach Harvest Size			
			2 to 3 months	6 months	1 year	2+ years
Broiler (meat chicken)	X		X			
Cattle Beef/Dairy		X				X
Dairy Goat	X				X	
Hen	X			X		
Pig				X (depending on breed)		
Rabbit	X		X			
Sheep	X				X	

OTHER CONSIDERATIONS

Cost of Getting Started

The larger the animal, the larger the upfront cost. A baby chick (depending on breed) will cost an average of three dollars, whereas a beef calf can be five hundred dollars. When talking beef cattle, the price, of course, can vary greatly based on location, breed, demand, and other factors, but that's a fair average at the time of this writing. Not only can the cost of getting said livestock vary, but generally, the larger the animal, the larger your feed bill and infrastructure costs.

Not only does it cost a lot more to feed a cow than a chicken, but you need a larger area to store their feed.

How Much Feed Per Animal

Ruminant Animals (Cattle, Bison, Goats, and Sheep)

How much to feed each animal will depend upon the weight of the animal (obviously older, larger animals eat more per day). The amount you need to purchase will vary based upon the available pasture, grass, or forage growing on your land for the time of year.

Ruminant animals are those with multiple chambers to their stomach, and they require a large amount of roughage and fiber. The general rule of thumb is that a ruminant animal requires 2.5 percent of their body weight in dry feed forage a day.

In other words, a 1,000-pound cow will consume about 25 pounds of dry weight forage per day. Remember that grass hay has some moisture content, so to meet the dry weight, you'll need to calculate the moisture content and add that additional weight to find your final feeding number. For example:

1,000 pound cow × 2.5% [0.025] = 25 pounds of dry weight forage
Grass hay is approximately 8% moisture content, so:
25 pounds × 8% [0.08] = 2 pounds
So your final calculation would be:
25 pounds dry + 2 pounds water weight = 27 pounds per day

Estimate some of the hay will be wasted and round it up to about 30 pounds per day.

We predominantly feed haylage, which averages a moisture content of 40 percent, so our daily amount based upon a 1,000 pound cow is 25 pounds × 40% (0.40) = 10 pounds. Add 25 pounds plus 10 pounds and we should feed each cow 35 pounds a day with an additional few pounds for waste.

Pigs

Again, how much to feed a pig per day depends upon their weight. A rough estimate is 4 percent of their body weight a day. A 100-pound pig would require 4 pounds of feed per day. You want to ensure they're also getting proper protein amounts (which vary by their age).

Animals eat more in cold weather to maintain body heat, so calculate extra if you're keeping them through the winter months.

Chickens

This depends on if you're raising meat birds or hens for eggs. Each has different feed requirements based on their age. (Noticing a theme here?)

According to the University of Kentucky Agriculture Extension Office,[6] a flock of 25 meat birds weighing 5 pounds at butcher time will go through five fifty-pound bags of feed.

If your hens don't have access to free-range forage, a good rule of thumb is to feed them one-quarter to one-third pound of feed per chicken per day. If they are free ranging or in a portable chicken tractor, you can scale this amount back.

Fencing

Cattle do well with both electric and barbed wire fencing. We use barbed wire for the perimeter, as we have close to fifteen acres to fence, and a lot of that is filled with underbrush, which will short out electric fencing. There is also the cost of running an electric fence, but there are solar units available to help

---

6 Jacquie Jacob and Tony Pescatore, "How Much Will My Chickens Eat?" University of Kentucky College of Agriculture, Food and Environment, accessed March 15, 2023, http://www2.ca.uky.edu/agcomm /pubs/ASC/ASC191/ASC191.pdf.

with the cost of electricity. We use Premier 1 electric poultry fencing with their solar battery as well as their electric fencing for our cattle for when we're sectioning off smaller grazing areas. We have been highly impressed by both.

Barbed wire is best used on permanent areas of fencing, though it can be taken out if needed. You'll need fence posts, of course. The two most common are metal T-posts that you pound into the ground and wooden fence posts. Wooden fence posts require digging a hole. If you're doing just a few, a manual post hole digger works fine, but for long stretches of fence you'll want to investigate renting a tractor with a hole digger on the back. When choosing wood, make sure you choose a variety that won't rot quickly, such as cedar or railroad ties. There are split rail fences made entirely of wood, but most people don't have access to that much wood or enough money to put in miles of this kind of fencing.

One note on barbed wire: If a cow can get their head through the wire, the rest of the body can and often will follow. We use four strands of wire for our fence. Make sure a strand is low enough to the ground that the cow can't crawl under it. They do a mean belly crawl. The top strand is best at about four feet, making it harder for a cow to jump over. (Though we've had some cows that must have been bred to a gazelle, because they jumped and cleared over four feet with room to spare.)

Between posts, metal fence stays are a good option to put in the middle of fence sections. A fence stay is a piece of twisted metal that keeps the wire from stretching when it's pushed or pulled.

Electric fencing works well for pigs and horses. Cattle will also respect an electric fence. You need to make sure the fence is properly grounded and that no grass or other items are touching it, as this can cause the fence to short out.

No matter which type of fencing you choose, you'll still need to monitor it regularly and check for weakened areas, loose posts, or holes in the fence.

The main reason cattle get out of a fence is to get to fresh feed. If they don't have enough to eat and there is ample food just on the other side of the fence, they will go for the greener grass. If you have a bull nearby and a cow goes into heat, nature will take over and he will come calling, fence or no fence.

Water

Clean and ample water is more important than food. Be sure to check water levels daily in hot weather. An automatic stock tank valve will keep your water tank at a certain level—you just connect your hose to the device. And a stock tank heater keeps water from freezing during frigid winter temperatures. An old bathtub makes an excellent water tank, and many times can be found for free when people are remodeling or renovating.

Breeding

With any livestock, you'll need to decide if you want to get into breeding or if you'd rather purchase animals to replace those you butcher for food. When possible, we prefer to buy our animals from someone we know, in order to see the conditions of the farm and ask questions.

We breed our cows every year. There are three options for breeding: artificial insemination, having your own bull, or taking your cow to a bull. If you only have a few cattle, having a bull will likely be more of a cost than it's worth. That is the case for us. Because my father has a herd of about 30 cows, he keeps a bull. We take our cows down to his bull when we're ready to have them bred.

We don't breed our own chickens or pigs. I purchase our pigs from a local breeder and in earlier years we received all our laying hens from friends who were thinning their flocks. We recently expanded our poultry flocks to ducks, who do incredibly well with our wet climate, eat slugs (our chickens won't touch a slug), give us eggs, and are about the cutest things to ever waddle their way through our homestead.

While breeding is more self-sufficient, be sure you're ready to take on all that caring for a pregnant mother and babies entails, as well as managing the male breeding animal. Oftentimes the male is more aggressive, as with bulls, roosters, and bucks (male goats). It is their job to protect their flock or herd, and occasionally, there is one who is really aggressive.

When I was a little girl, we had a bull who would charge people when they were in the field. We hadn't had him very long, and none of our other bulls behaved like this. I was used to walking along the fence line in the pasture to go visit my grandma, who lived up the field from us. I had worn a trail in the grass and under the fence where I'd slide through into her yard.

One day I was walking in the field with my mom and a few of the neighborhood kids. I was the last one and dawdling in the field. My mom and the others had made it back through the fence into the yard. All of a sudden my mother and the other kids started yelling. "Run! Get out of the way!"

I stood there, not having a clue what they were all hollering about. Slowly, I looked over my shoulder.

The bull was barreling toward me. His hooves pounded the dirt.

Fear rushed through my veins. The screams of my mom finally registered. I sprinted for the fence.

The bull was removed from our homestead promptly.

We've had other bulls who were like pets. My father could walk up and pet them and they followed him through the long grass like a dog. When owning livestock, you'll definitely want to observe the behavior of the animals before bringing them home and make sure your fences or pens are strong enough to hold them.

BEEF

Most folks aren't able to raise their own beef. After all, it does require some property. As I mentioned, we plan for an acre or two of pasture per animal to avoid feeding them hay all year long. If you don't have property, leasing pasture from someone else is an option. Some farmers will allow you to purchase a cow from them and have you pay a certain amount for them to raise it for you. Another option is to just purchase the beef at butchering time for a set-upon amount per pound. This is the most common method where we are.

You can find small farmers who sell a whole, half, or quarter of a beef each fall. Ask friends who they purchase from or if they know of anyone who has extra to sell. Social media makes this extremely easy, as multiple people can answer and point you in the right direction at once. If you live near us in Washington, we offer this!

PIGS

Pigs are a good alternative to cattle if you have less land but still want a large amount of meat while only raising a few animals. We've found it's the same amount of work to raise two pigs as it is to raise one, and it keeps them from being lonely.

If you get your piglets when the nights are still cold, you'll need to keep them under a heat lamp for the first couple of weeks. We've raised pigs in the winter and spring and it's definitely less work when they're raised during the warmer months.

Piglets will need some sort of shelter from the weather. We used an old crate and turned it on its side with a tarp over the top and sides to create a dry and shady area. Pigs don't sweat, so it's also important for them to have a way to keep cool during the hotter months. This is why pigs like to wallow in mud holes—it helps cool them off. Our pigs love to play in the water and will jump into the water trough until just their snouts are sticking out. If you spray water out of the hose, they'll run through it like a couple of kids in a sprinkler.

Pigs also like to root, so they'll quickly plow any area they're penned up in. If you have an area of ground you want worked up for a new garden plot or to get rid of brush, consider putting part of your pig pen there so the pigs can dig up the vegetation with their snouts. You'll also receive free fertilizer in the form of their manure.

When they're small, you'll want to use wire mesh fencing. Once they're older (big enough that they won't walk right under the bottom strand), you can use barbed wire fencing. However, they can root down and under the fence, so you'll want to run a strand of hot wire along the bottom of the fence near the ground.

Pigs love fruit and vegetables. We plant extra summer and winter squash to feed our pigs and roast a couple of large zucchini in the summer to feed them each day. Instead of a grain- or corn-based diet, we feed our pigs vegetables, barley, and even hay. When the apples come on, we pick up all the fallen ones from our neighbors' and family's trees. We think it gives the meat a sweeter flavor.

Pigs will eat any table scraps, but we don't feed them anything with meat in it. While our pigs don't have as much fat on them as corn-fed pigs, the taste in the meat is well worth it. They like bread as well, but just as with people, a diet rich in vegetables and fruit is best.

Check with your local grocery stores for produce that is beyond its prime. Many will allow you to come and pick up unsalable items. If you have any farms nearby, you might also check with them for unsalable produce. Now, you don't want to be feeding your pigs rotten food. The meat will taste like what they've been fed. But slightly past prime is fine.

CHICKENS

I've heard it said that chickens are a gateway animal to wanting a full-on farm. Like many things in life, I went at this backward. We started out with cattle, raised pigs, and then added chickens.

If you'd like to try your hand at chickens and you live within city limits, you'll need to check out city ordinances. Many cities will allow you to have a few chickens, but you'll want to double-check for your area. You may also want to check with your neighbors if you live in close quarters. Most folks don't mind listening to chickens squawk (and they do) if they get a dozen free eggs from time to time. Think twice about a rooster. Squawking is one thing; a rooster crowing in the wee hours of the morning is quite another.

If you live out on a farm like us, you can get as many chickens as your heart desires . . . or as your patience allows. I recommend starting out with already-laying hens. You may pay a little bit more, but it's by far worth it in my opinion. Having raised two flocks, we've had much more success with purchasing older hens.

The chicks are cute. All the soft, downy fluffballs are sweet as they toddle about, but they're a lot more work. You must provide them with a heat lamp until their feathers come in. They don't begin to lay eggs until about four to five months old, so you'll be paying for feed and care without any eggs in return. Because they're young, they're more likely to get into trouble. Older hens are more cautious and watch out for predators.

Starting with already-laying hens also ensures you won't accidently end up with hens that have suddenly turned into roosters. I know many an unsuspecting person who has thought she was buying hens and ended up with four roosters by mistake. But if you plan on letting your hens hatch out baby chicks, then a rooster isn't such a bad idea. Roosters also tend to protect the flock.

However, roosters like to crow. I like to sleep in when I can. See the conflict?

Too many roosters will also lead to worn-out hens, and some people are bothered by fertilized chicken eggs. They will have blood spots in them if they're starting to develop baby chicks.

We choose not to have a rooster at this time.

Meat Chickens

Heritage breed chickens take longer to raise, resulting in a higher cost of feed and an older bird by the time they're ready to be butchered. This isn't all bad, as they're easier to come by and can be used for both eggs and meat.

White Cornish broilers are a hybrid chicken, meaning they've been raised specifically for meat and selectively bred (not genetically modified) for traits of growing quickly and having a lot of meat. They are ready to be butchered at just eight to ten weeks of age.

We decided to go with the White Cornish broilers due to their short raising period. You can either order chicks by mail or purchase them from a store in the spring. We've purchased our meat chicks from both a local feed store and a family-owned hatchery.

Exclusively for the past five years we've purchased our meat chickens, hens, and ducks from a family-run and operated hatchery, Murray McMurray. Baby chicks can be shipped through the mail at birth because when chicks hatch, they don't need food or water for the first three days of life. (In the wild, not all the eggs hatch at the same time. A hen can't leave her unhatched eggs to tend to the hatched chicks, or the rest of the chicks will die before hatching.) So hatcheries can ship out chicks on the day they're hatched even if they won't reach their destination for a couple of days.

You should call your post office to let them know your chicks are on their way so they can call you the moment the chicks arrive in the morning.

You'll need to provide some sort of coop for your chickens. They'll need nesting boxes and a place to roost. Plenty of clean water and feed is also necessary. Chickens love vegetable and fruit scraps, and they'll clean up your yard of bugs as well. But they might beat you to the ripe strawberries and tomatoes. They also like bread. Truthfully, they'll eat just about anything. You can help keep your feed bill down by supplementing with kitchen scraps and garden extras.

Chickens scratch, a lot, mainly the ground, but occasionally each other. They'll scratch a hole in your flowerbeds like a dog burying a bone. If you like manicured lawns and flowers, you won't want free-ranging chickens.

But for the work they require, there is nothing like farm-fresh eggs. Even the organic pasture-raised eggs you buy from the store don't compare to the eggs straight from your own backyard. The yolks are a deep orange and I swear they taste better.

When my chickens went through their molting period this past fall and didn't lay eggs for a month, I had to purchase eggs from the store. It had been years since I bought eggs, and when I cracked one open and saw a pale yellow yolk, I stared at it in confusion for a moment. *This isn't how eggs are supposed to look*, I thought.

I whispered a prayer of thanks when my girls started laying faithfully again. My baked goods returned to their normal richer color and flavor.

When left to free range, our chickens especially like to be wherever we are. They talk. A lot. I've been known to carry on a good conversation or two myself, but our chickens can out-talk even me.

TEN TIPS FOR RAISING MEAT CHICKENS

1. **Inspect before you buy.** If you are purchasing from a store, be sure you see the chicks up and walking before loading them up. We had a chick one year that had a broken leg. It was lying down when we purchased it and we didn't see the injury until we got home. It died within a day.

2. **Have a heat lamp ready.** When chicks only have their down, they need a heat lamp to keep warm. They'll need the heat lamp until their feathers come in, usually about three weeks with meat birds. It's also important to have them in a pen or area without corners. Chicks can become trapped in corners and trampled by the other birds.

3. **Be prepared to feed a lot.** If you're used to raising regular laying hens, be prepared to feed meat chickens much more often and use a lot more feed. Our hens will go through their feed in about four days. The meat chickens went through the same amount in a day. Take away their feed at night to help establish healthy eating habits and avoid organ failure.

4. **Keep the water full.** Just like their feed, they go through a lot more water. Be sure they have plenty of fresh water in their pen.

5. **Only dish up healthy feed.** Be sure and purchase only unmedicated feed for your chickens. We purchased organic feed to be sure they weren't getting GMO products in their food. Remember, you're going to be eating what they're eating.

6. **Be sure they have shade.** Their feathers are slower to come in and they have light skin. If you let them out into a run or pasture, keep food and water in the coop and where they're ranging.

7. **Keep their pens clean.** Don't stuff your birds into a tiny living area. Be sure they have room to move about. It's best for them to run around on pasture. If that's not possible, be sure there's enough space for them to spread out and for you to keep it clean. Also be sure there is adequate ventilation.

8. **Don't back out.** Once you have the meat chickens, do not change your mind about butchering them. They're bred to be raised to a maximum of ten weeks. If you go over this, their legs will break and give out due to the weight of their bodies. Or they'll have heart failure. The whole point of raising your own meat is to be humane. Don't let them suffer because you got cold feet.

9. **Mark the calendar.** Count out from when you purchased the chickens to their full maturity date of eight to ten weeks. Many county extension offices have chicken butchering equipment for rent at reasonable rates, but you'll have to reserve it in advance.

10. **Don't become attached.** Anytime we're raising animals for food, we don't think of them as pets. We don't name them. We do make sure they're cared for and treated humanely. Our children know upfront the animals are for food. We don't lie, fib, or try to hide the fact. Our children are very well adjusted to the reality that we raise our own food, and they know what that entails.

CHAPTER 8

BE PREPARED:
EMERGENCY PROVISIONS

Making a plan for energy and power provisions is one of the most important things you can do for your farm or home. This is my surge of tips for you for both everyday efficiency and for any emergency you may face. I provide a checklist at the end to help you get organized and set a plan right away.

EVERYDAY EFFICIENCY

Unplug items not in use. You know how you can walk through your home in the middle of the night and see all kinds of green, red, and blue appliance lights blinking at you? Those glowing lights are all drawing power. I put all the electronics at my desk and in our family room on a power strip. Whenever they're not in use, I flip off the power strip, eliminating phantom power.
Reuse items. So many things can be used again and again. I rinse out plastic storage and freezer bags and dry them to use later. Butter wrappers are excellent to use for greasing a pan. Cut up old towels into cleaning rags or use old socks as a cleaning mitt. Parchment paper is one of my favorite baking tools. I can reuse the same piece of parchment paper to bake bread up to five times. Almost anything in our homes can be put to another purpose!
Run things during nonpeak hours. Most power companies charge a different rate per hour during nonpeak and peak hours. I try to run our dishwasher, washing machine, and dryer (when weather inhibits the clothesline) during

nonpeak hours. Nonpeak hours are often from 8:00 a.m. to 8:00 p.m., excluding weekends. Contact your power company for exact hours and rates.

Check your thermostat. Last time the power went out, it somehow reset our thermostat. I got quite a shock when our electric bill came. Now I check it frequently. Just a couple of degrees can make a big difference. My husband is a sawyer so we have access to firewood. With the frequent power outages, we heat our home with a wood-burning stove. In fact, when the thermostat on our electric heat broke two years ago, we decided to forego spending the money to fix it and chose to rely solely on our woodstove. Since then, we've had some of the coldest winters on record here, single digit lows, but our woodstove has kept us warm. We have no plans to repair the electric heat.

GENERATORS

Consider having a backup generator. One of the best investments we've ever made is our generator. For years, we had a small generator and we alternated its use between the fridge and freezer, and we could also run the coffee pot, a lamp, and the television. However, we are on a private well, and it wasn't large enough to run the well, which meant no running water when the power was out.

A few years ago, we decided to upgrade to a generator that could power both the entire house (with the exception of the hot water tank) and the well at the same time.

Do You Need a Generator?

Here are some things to consider:

1. What are your must-have items that will need power during a power outage?
2. If you have livestock, you also need to consider them. Do you need lights for smaller animals to keep them warm? Do you need power so you can get water for your animals?
3. How often, on average, are you without power?

What Size Generator Do You Need?

Having a generator large enough to power all your needs is crucial, so knowing the wattage of your appliances and other "must-have" electrical items is key to knowing what generator is right for you. Armed with this information, look at the watts on the generators you're considering. Do not look at the maximum watts. This tells you that you can pull up to a maximum amount of wattage from the generator. Instead, look at the average running watts. This is the amount of wattage that the generator can actually power at any given time.

Using a Generator

If at all possible, I'd recommend you have your generator set up on a transfer switch. We had an electrician come out to our house and set up our breaker box so we had the capability of flipping a switch that would then power our entire home from the generator at the breaker box (no extension cords other than the one from the generator to the box). Here are some other things to remember.

1. Make sure all breakers are labeled so you can easily turn off breakers that will draw too much power.
2. Label all breakers, both in the house and outside at your box if you have more than one building or power source running from it.
3. Never use a generator indoors. Not only are they incredibly loud but they can be lethal due to carbon monoxide poisoning! You need proper ventilation.
4. If the power is out due to a storm, wait until the storm is over (or until it's safe) to set up your generator.
5. Make sure all breakers are turned off both at your electric box and at the generator when you first power it up. Let it run for a few minutes to warm up.
6. Next, plug in your main generator plug to the plug at the box (if you have it wired in). Make sure you line it up and turn it to lock it into place.

7. Then, turn on the breaker to the appliance that uses the most power first. For us, this is the breaker to our pump house and well. That allows it to draw and kick on first without bogging down the motor. Once that has had a chance to fire up, then we turn on the other breakers for the rest of the house (except for the hot tub and hot water tank).
8. If your generator runs out of fuel, let it cool down before refueling it.
9. Quality extension cords matter, especially when you are running power through multiple cords to reach all areas of your home that need power.

When we had a smaller generator, we would set it up outside on our back porch. From the generator, we would run a long extension cord into the house via a back window and we'd plug in a power strip to that cord.

Then we would plug an extension cord into our deep freezer that's near our kitchen, and another extension cord into our refrigerator, and we'd alternate plugging those into the power strip (because our generator wasn't powerful enough to power both at the same time).

We would also have a few plugs left open on the power strip for things like the coffee pot, toaster, TV, etc. to get us through the outage.

Our old generator wasn't strong enough to power our electric cookstove, my computer, our well, or our hot water tank, so we would predominantly cook on the wood stove during a power outage.

After going through a two-week power outage when there was a mudslide in our area, we upgraded to a DuroMax XP12000EH. This is a propane or gas-powered generator that's also RV-ready.

EMERGENCY PREPAREDNESS

There are many different aspects to preparedness and one section can't give in-depth coverage to them all. However, the following pages of charts and worksheets will allow you to determine which items are most vital and important to your family and allow you to track if you have them or if you need to purchase them.

Emergency and Preparedness for Peace of Mind

Item		Qty on Hand		Tier
Air horn				
Alternate methods for cooking, camp stove				
Alternate methods for cooking, charcoal grill				
Alternate methods for cooking, fire pit				
Alternate methods for cooking, propane grill				
Alternate methods for cooking, rocket stove				
Alternate methods for cooking, solar oven				
Alternate methods for cooking, wonder oven				
Animal first aid kits				
Bathtub water storage liner				
Baton or bat				
Battery bank				
Battery charger				
Blankets, extra				
Bug-Out bag				
Can opener, manual				
Cards				
Cast-iron cookware				
Charcoal				
Cold-weather coats				

Item	Qty on Hand		Tier
Compass			
Containers for collecting water			
Containers for storing water			
Containers for transporting water			
Coolers for cold food			
Escape ladder for upstairs windows			
Extra sump pump			
Extra water for animals			
Extra water for cleaning and hygiene			
Extra water for drinking			
Extra well pump			
Extra work boots/footwear			
Firewood			
Flares			
Flashlight, crank			
Food chopper, manual			
Games			
Glow sticks			
Gun: handgun			
Gun: handgun ammunition			

Item	Qty on Hand		Tier
Gun: handgun extra magazines			
Gun: rifle			
Gun: rifle ammunition			
Gun: rifle extra magazines			
Hand Crank Emergency Radio			
Hand and foot warmers			
Hats, gloves, thermal underwear			
Headlamps			
Hunting knife with gut hook			
Insulated boots			
Kitchen timer, no battery			
Lanterns			
Lighter fluid			
Machete			
Maps of local area (not digital)			
Mosquito net			
Motion detector perimeter lights			
Multifunction tool			
Pepper spray (compact & bear)			
Portable solar charger			

Item	Qty on Hand	Tier
Puzzle books		
Puzzles		
Rain poncho		
Rechargeable batteries		
Sleeping bags		
Snare kit		
Sterno		
Sunglasses		
Tent		
Thermos for hot food		
Totable toilet (stocked with supplies)		
Utility wrench		
Walkie-talkies		
Water bottles		
Water purifier, bleach		
Water purifier, distiller		
Water purifier, filters		
Water siphon		
Waterproof matches		
Whistle		
Wool socks		

Special Needs

Item		Qty on Hand		Tier
Battery-powered version of medical equipment				
Cane or walker for walking assistance (extra)				
Chew necklace or pencil toppers				
Dentures, extra				
Fidget toy				
Footwear, prescription (extra)				
Hearing aid/amplifier (extra)				
Light filters				
List of doctors and numbers				
List of health history				
List of medications and dosage				
List of vitamins and dosage				
Mood bands				
Noise-cancelling headphones				
Pencil grips				
Sensory toys				
Sitting wedge or wobble cushion				
Special dietary foods and supplies				
Special supplies: sharps container				
Special supplies: ventilator				

Item		Qty on Hand		Tier
Visually impaired: glasses, magnifiers, talking or braille clock				
Visual timer				
Weighted blanket				
Weighted lap pad or vest				

Documents (have these in one place to grab quickly)

Item	Qty on Hand	Tier
Birth certificates		
Copy of deeds		
Copy of driver's license		
Copy of immunization records		
Copy of insurance policies		
Copy of passports		
Copy of Social Security cards		
Copy of stocks and bonds		
Copy of will		
Death certificates		
Emergency numbers		
Family and friends: addresses/phone numbers		
Important telephone numbers		
Inventory of valuable household goods		
Marriage certificates		
Pictures of family members		
Record of bank account numbers		
Record of credit card account numbers and companies' contact information		

Additional Documents

Item	Qty on Hand	Tier

ACKNOWLEDGMENTS

The writing and birthing of a book is just as much a story as the book itself. There have been many individuals who helped write on the pages of my life and are a part of my story. My thanks to all these people and many more . . .

To my husband and children. I'm blessed beyond words by you. Thank you for your love and support.

To my mother, who read to me every night from the time I can remember. You instilled a love of books in me long before either of us knew what it would lead to.

To my father, who taught me the value of hard work. Your memories and knowledge of the old ways ensure they won't be forgotten and are passed on to others.

To Colleen L. Reece. If it weren't for your seeing the potential in my writing, I would have given up this dream forever. Thank you for following God's leading and your red editor's pen.

To Anne Schwartz. Thank you for sharing your gardening expertise and dedicating your work to being a good steward of the land and teaching others about organic practices.

To all my readers who have sent notes of encouragement, stories, or just saying hello. I'm honored you let me be a part of your lives.

To my heavenly Father. Thank You for drawing me to You and for Your mercy and grace.

RECIPE INDEX

Preserving Recipes

From-Scratch Cooking

Homemade Cleaners

Quick Reference Lists

INSPIRING YOUR FAITH AND PIONEER ROOTS

If you love old-fashioned living and think we need to get back to the simple way of life, then my *Pioneering Today* podcast is for you. We'll talk about how our great-grandparents lived and how to capture that in our modern lives.

The *Pioneering Today* podcast is where food is homegrown, Mason jars line our pantries, meals are made from scratch, and the soul is nourished. The bimonthly podcast is dedicated to helping you integrate the best of the pioneer lifestyle into your modern one. I hope you'll be inspired to grow your own food; cook real, traditional meals; increase your home food storage; consider livestock; and draw closer in your relationship with Jesus.

Subscribe at MelissaKNorris.com

If you are inspired to make some small or big changes, I would love to continue to encourage you. I created a free five-day fast track Made-From-Scratch Life e-course as my way of saying thank you for purchasing this book and spending your precious time with me. Simply sign up here: melissaknorris.com/book/the-made-from-scratch-life

Over five days you'll get five e-mails from me with tips and articles on how to implement these changes into your life and kitchen without being overwhelmed. We'll have some fun inspiration and a thing or two involving Mason jars . . . because I just can't help myself when it comes to Mason jars.

I can't wait to meet you and hear about your transformations!

Connect with Melissa online!

facebook.com/MelissaKNorris

@MelissaKNorris

pinterest.com/MelissaKNorris

MEET MELISSA

MELISSA K. NORRIS inspires people's faith and pioneer roots with old-fashioned skill sets and wisdom featured in her books, podcast, and blog. Melissa lives with her husband and two children on their 15-acre homestead in Washington state. She and her family are also revitalizing a 40-acre farmstead as a teaching farm.

SHARE THE ABUNDANCE OF THE GARDEN WITH YOUR LOVED ONES

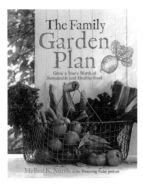

Do something good for your family by planting a garden that will yield healthy, wholesome fruits and vegetables throughout the year. Learn the entire process, from planning your crops and garden space to harvesting and preserving the food you grow.

This indispensable guide includes everything you need to plan your garden, execute your plan, and record your results, saving you time and hassle—and allowing you to have fun with the process. Grow healthy produce for your family all year long.

Discover these and other homesteading resources at MelissaKNorris.com.